MEN *of* POWER

Also by Jim Hohnberger

Escape to God

Empowered Living

It's About People

Come to the Quiet

JIM HOHNBERGER

MEN *of* POWER

RECLAIMING YOUR LEGACY

Pacific Press® Publishing Association
Nampa, Idaho
Oshawa, Ontario, Canada
www.pacificpress.com

Cover design by Mark Bond
Inside design by Steve Lanto
Cover photo © iStockphoto.com

A note to the reader: Every experience shared in this volume is true, although, in a few cases, multiple individuals have been combined into one character for sake of brevity and clarity. In most cases, the names, locations, and other unimportant characteristics have been altered to protect the privacy of the individuals involved. Outside of those whose names and stories have been used with their permission, resemblance to any person or persons, outside of the author and his family, is strictly coincidental.

Unless otherwise noted, all Scripture quotations are from the King James Version of the Bible.
Scripture quotations attributed to NKJV are from the Holy Bible, The New King James Version, copyright © 1979, 1980, 1982 by Thomas Nelson, Inc. Used by permission.
Scripture quotations attributed to NIV are from the HOLY BIBLE, NEW INTERNATIONAL VERSION, copyright © 1973, 1978, 1984 International Bible Society. Used by permission of Zondervan Bible Publishers.
Scripture quotations attributed to TLB are from *The Living Bible*, copyright © 1971 by Tyndale House Publishers, Wheaton, Ill. Used by permission.
Scripture quotations attributed to Phillips are from J. B. Phillips: *The New Testament in Modern English,* Revised Edition, copyright © J. B. Phillips 1958, 1960, 1972. Used by permission of Macmillan Publishing Co., Inc.
Scripture quotations from *The Message.* Copyright © by Eugene H. Peterson 1993, 1994, 1995. Used by permission of NavPress Publishing Group.

ISBN 13: 978-0-8163-2191-9
ISBN 10: 0–8163–2191-4

Additional copies of this book are available by calling toll-free 1-800-765-6955 or by visiting http://www.adventistbookcenter.com.

07 08 09 10 11 • 5 4 3 2 1

Dedication

If you find yourself floundering in your personal life, if your marriage has gone stale and your children have lost respect for you, this book has been written to place in your hand the key to reclaiming all you have lost. This book is for you!

Acknowledgment

Few of us are ten-talent people. It took more talent than I possess to complete *Men of Power*. Special thanks to my personal assistant, Jeanette Houghtelling, who so thoughtfully, prayerfully, and skillfully applied her God-given ability to enhance and enlarge *Men of Power*.

Table of Contents

A Note to the Reader

Every man has a legacy—a heritage of real manhood. However, far too many of us men find that legacy elusive. We're not sure what the legacy is, much less how to reclaim it. Consequently, we've pursued myths, settled for substitutes, or pretended all is well when deep inside, something is missing.

The simple principles you will find in this book, when consistently applied, will provide that "missing something." You will find that they will not only revitalize any marriage and reconnect any family but will also empower you to be a real man—the man that God designed you to be.

Regardless of your past and irrespective of your present circumstances, you can become a man of power. Go ahead and reclaim your legacy.

In Search
of Men

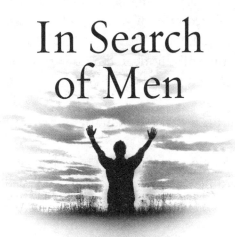

I sought for a man among them . . . but I found none.
—Ezekiel 22:30

Not long ago, my family and I were flying overseas for a series of speaking engagements. The flight was well underway when a big screen came down, and there for our entertainment was the latest James Bond film featuring Agent 007. I recalled having seen the poster for this very movie at the grocery store just a few days before, and I realized that we were about to witness a portrait of the macho man. You've seen him—the insensitive brute who cares for no one but himself. The man who displays tenderness only when he can use it to get what he wants. The man who can follow the base dictates of his flesh and say his conscience doesn't bother him. Is that a real man?

Since we fly quite often, we had come prepared with reading material to occupy our minds. I tried to read and concentrate, but you can only stare at your lap for so long before your eyes unwillingly snatch a movement or two from the screen. These scenes have a nearly irresistible force drawing your attention. As I sat there thinking about how I had raised my two boys, my indignation began to rise. I had always tried to give them the best and guard them from all the rest. Now, before them was this perverted picture of manhood. Even though they were doing an admirable job of ignoring the film, I decided I wasn't going to sit by and allow this situation to go unchallenged.

I went looking for the head flight attendant and shared with her how my wife and I were dedicated to raising our sons to have wholesome passions based on the life of Christ and His Word. "Would you, for their sakes, please turn off this degrading portrayal of a man?"

She shrugged her shoulders. "Sir, I can do nothing; I'm just a flight attendant."

"Then will you please call the captain and share my concerns with him?" I urged.

She did, and he suggested, "Call the president of the airlines."

I vowed I would do that just as soon as we landed and could get to our destination.

Where are the men?

My disturbed thoughts turned to Judy, an attractive young lady who had come to me at one of my seminars. "Something is wrong with men these days!" she had exclaimed. "I'd like to get married, but I've looked and I've looked for a real man—a godly man, a man I could consider giving my heart to—and I can't find any! *What has happened to all the men*, Mr. Hohnberger?"

It's a solemn question and one that God asks as well. In every age, He searches for men—real men who are willing to accept their divine calling, men who recognize the fast-eroding state of their nation and their families, and who will boldly stand for the right, saying, *"No more!"* Can't you hear the longing in God's words as He agonized over exiled Judah? "I sought for a man among them, that should make up the hedge, and stand in the gap before me for the land, that I should not destroy it: but I found none."[1]

If God could have found just one man . . . but there were no men fortifying their families from the rising tide of sin; no men protecting their loved ones, placing a hedge between them and the flood of iniquity prevailing in their society and in their church; no men raising up the next generation of real men for virtuous young ladies like Judy to fall in love with.

I don't believe the situation today is any better than it was in the time of Ezekiel; if anything, it is worse. Where are the men today? Why

---

1. Ezekiel 22:30.

are the families, even of those men in the church, being spoiled by the prevailing evil about them? Why do young ladies, seeking for the highest and noblest of manly virtues, find their search so difficult?

The answer is simple. It has been sitting in the Gospel of Mark for two thousand years, and we have missed it. "No man can enter into a strong man's house, and spoil his goods, *except he will first bind the strong man; and then he will spoil his house.*"[2] It is happening today—not in just a few homes, but in almost every home. The devil has broken down the door to our homes and is spoiling our goods. He is taking our children captive through the influence of their associates, TV, music, and the Internet. The result is that our children and youth think like, talk like, act like, and look just like the world about them. And the devil doesn't quit there. He sneaks in the back door and corrupts our wives. Slowly but surely, their affections are entwined about the world until they become like Lot's wife.[3]

And why is he so successful in spoiling our goods? Because he has bound the strong men. He has bound us with lies, with myths, with false portraits of manhood until we are like King Saul and his army cowering in tents while Goliath spews out blasphemies against the living God. Where are the patriarchs, like young David, who will kneel before God in humble submission and then go out to face Goliath in the name of the Lord and vindicate His cause?

We men of today don't realize we have been lured away from our post of duty and bound with chains. We don't recognize that we have been tricked into devaluing our most precious treasures. We have been told that we must accept the Goliaths in our lives as unconquerable and look upon evil as normal. Hence, we unquestioningly accept the damage being done.

But that's the bad news. Here's the good news! God doesn't throw us out! Instead, He longs to empower us to break our bands. He is waiting to train us to take up our posts of duty. He wants to strengthen us to resist the evil about us so that it doesn't shut us in like a cloud. He is capable of transforming us from pansies to patriarchs. Therefore, none of us should be discouraged.

---

2. Mark 3:27, italics added.
3. See Genesis 19:26.

FAMILIAR FASCINATION

On that flight, I was restless and decided to walk the aisles and observe the reactions of the four-hundred-plus passengers. It appeared to me that 80 percent of those on the flight were adults—men and women in equal proportions—and that the rest were children of various ages. Whether children or adults, the majority—maybe 85 percent—had their eyes glued to the screen, living out vicariously the exploits of what just might be Hollywood's epitome of the macho man—a man who is cool and smooth, someone to be admired and emulated. I ask, "Since when is it cool to murder, fornicate, lie, and mow over anyone who gets in your way?"

Is this why our young boys walk around with guns and knives like Agent 007? Then they carry a weapon to school and shoot and murder at will—and we wonder why! We wonder why nobody can control them. It is because we have left our post of duty, men! Our boys have no sentinels to say, "The enemy is before you!"

Instead, as I walked the length of that plane, I saw a familiar fascination in the eyes and passions of those passengers. Familiar, I say, because there was a time in my life I would have done just what they were doing. I especially took notice of the men, with their wives and children by their side, passively and pleasurably taking in the scenes, seemingly oblivious to the destructive ideas being injected into their minds. I inwardly recoiled as men allowed their sons to see women exploited as mere objects and to view drinking, smoking, gambling, and killing as manly activities. Their daughters saw women shamelessly using their sexuality to achieve their ends as if this were acceptable and honorable behavior. Doesn't anyone realize that *by beholding we become changed*— changed into the same image? The advertising industry knows that; why are we so naive?

Then I began to look more closely at those who *weren't* watching the movie, thinking that maybe some of them were as disgusted as I was. But most of those not watching were sleeping, oblivious to everything about them. Somehow, it seemed an appropriate analogy, for so many men sleep through all the warnings, all the early signs of trouble, and are taken unaware when their marriage or children suddenly face a crisis.

I came across one man thumbing through a copy of *Sports Illustrated* between glances at the movie, as though sex and murder bored him terribly. At last, I saw a well-dressed man, clearly engrossed in reading. *Ah, here,* I thought, *is a man not willing to be corrupted by the filth on the screen. He's totally focused upon something else!* Then as I walked past, I saw he was engrossed in a girlie magazine. Heavy-hearted, I headed back to my seat. On the way I found one more man reading—one of the supermarket tabloids.

I plopped back down in my seat disturbed about where we, as a society, are headed. Evil is increasing. Immorality of all types is not only becoming common but demands to be viewed as normal. Our society is increasingly preyed upon by pedophiles, with real-life murder and commonplace abortions devaluing human life. What hope is there for boys growing up now?

Judgmental?

Some well-meaning folk have cautioned me against drawing conclusions based upon other people's personal tastes and preferences. I ask: "Why not?" We make evaluations all the time about what we see, and it is important that we do so! A person's outward appearance tells much about the inner life.

When we see a dog foaming at the mouth, snarling and attacking anyone or anything in its path, do we disregard the outward evidence of an inward problem and walk up to scratch his head? It is absolute folly to think that our choices for conduct somehow exist in a vacuum and that no one should draw value judgments based upon them. Anyone who has ever gone to a job interview knows how ridiculous this idea is.

Part of the reason why the Christian church is no longer an immoveable bulwark against the rising tide of compromise is that Christians have bought into this false concept. The fear of being labeled "judgmental" overrides the fear of God and real concern for the well-being of others—or perhaps our own love for compromise seals our lips from speaking against it. I thought about the well-known television evangelists, some of whom seem to care more for gold, for glory, or for girls than they do for God. Should that alert us that there is a problem of the heart? Or do we sit by complacently?

HELP!

My heart sank as I remembered my own search for a pastor—any pastor—who could help me solve the dilemma I faced at one point in my personal life. After I accepted the Word of God as the sole rule of my life, I joined a conservative church. I made many lifestyle changes, and consequently most people considered me a born-again Christian. But I still had a huge problem—my German temper! There seemed to be more Hitler in me than Luther. You see, in public, I was the polite businessman. In church, I was the religious elder. In social gatherings, I was somewhat the life of the party. But at home, this German temper came out—especially if my lovely wife crossed me. Here, I was power-less.

I went to my pastor and said, "I need help. When I get home at the end of a long, stressful day, I'll come in the back door, and my wife will sweetly say, 'Mr. Smith called, dear.' "

" 'What did he want?' I inquire.

" 'I don't know. I didn't ask him,' she innocently replies.

"My flesh rises in irritation as I point my finger at her, raise my voice, and interrogate, 'Why didn't you ask him?'

" 'I didn't think of it,' she responds, cringing.

" 'When will you ever learn to *think?*' I drill into her. And so it goes, week after week. I've given up so many of my former ways—the drinking, swearing, dancing, movies, bars, and gambling—but this temper. Surely you can help me here."

I shared my dilemma with six different pastors. I found out they all had the same problem I did. I was dumbstruck. Pastors, are you telling me there's grace sufficient for all my former ways—except my temper behind closed doors with my family? No one could help me. How could the shepherds of the flock not have a practical solution to such a univer-sal problem?

SOMEONE'S GOT TO LEAD

Another tendency today is that men are abdicating many of their roles in society and allowing them to be filled by women. We may once have been a patriarchal society, but today, by default, we have become largely a matriarchal society. Women are now the dominant influence in our sons' lives. Women run our homes. At school, the overwhelming majority of our teachers are women. At church, we have women pastors, women elders, women deacons, and women Bible school teachers. Now I am not against women. Women *should* have a dynamic influence in the lives of our children. Many homes today are single-parent homes—single women raising children on their own. This is not ideal, but it is reality. But it is also reality that God never intended the influence of a woman to take the place of the influence He planned men to have in their homes and in society.

As the flight continued, I thought about other current trends. Many rock bands look and sing like the devil himself. And youth emulate the artists they idolize. Their hairstyles look like they stuck their finger in a light socket or got run over by a lawn mower. Their clothes state, "I'm bad." "I'm cool." "I don't care." "Slop is great." Where are the men who are blowing the whistle on the falsehoods so obvious in the lives and philosophy of such children? Who has the courage to say that it isn't cool to conform to group norm and dress in clothes a charity would be ashamed to give away? Who cares enough to prevent their daughters from dressing immodestly and cruising the shopping malls? Who's going to say "No" and enforce it when the youth want to smoke, drink, use drugs, or dance like the heathen tribes in old Tarzan movies? What has happened to the men in our society who knew right from wrong?

OLD DOC HILDEBRAND

I was seventeen when acute appendicitis hospitalized me. I had been smoking for some time because it was the manly thing to do (remember the Marlboro man?). Now, underage in the hospital, I snuck one whenever I could. In those days you could smoke almost anywhere, including the hospital, but I wasn't yet an adult, and when my doctor heard I was smoking he came up for a little chat.

"The nurses tell me you've been smoking."

"Well, yeah."

"You think it's manly to smoke?"

"Most men do."

"Well, if you're going to smoke like a man you need to learn to do it right and not hide the fact that you are smoking. Here," he commanded, pulling out a pack he'd bought for the occasion, "go ahead and smoke one."

Trapped, I determined not to be humiliated, so I lit up, but that wasn't quite good enough for old Doc Hildebrand. "Breath deeper, that's how a real man does it. Come on! Smoke another one. A man can light the next one from the remains of the last. Go on! Do it, Jimmy!"

I started sputtering and coughing, but he paid me no heed and kept badgering me and pushing me to smoke more and more until I was so sick I couldn't continue. I was coughing and gagging, and every movement was agonizing to my fresh abdominal incision. I was so sick and in so much pain I thought I was going to die! He glanced at me, nodded his head thoughtfully, and left without another word. I don't know how long I was sick, but it seemed like forever. As the intense spasms of sickness eased off, my stomach complained bitterly about the abuse it had just endured, and I had more pain than I had experienced up to this point, even right after the surgery. Finally I asked the nurse for some medication.

"Doctor Hildebrand said you were a real man and wouldn't need anything like that, so he canceled all your medication orders," she sweetly responded.

The next time Dr. Hildebrand checked in on me, I asked rather sheepishly, "Uh, Doc . . . do you think I could get some pain medicine for my stomach? It's really hurting me." He gazed at me for a long time as if reading my soul, and then, satisfied, he replied, "Sure, Jim, I think we could do that." He ordered some medication for me, and I never smoked another cigarette. I wish Dr. Hildebrand was still around to thank. I have been ever so grateful to him. His tough love saved my life. In those days, he was just an average man, but in comparison with today's men he stands a towering giant!

I sat in my airplane seat and sadly contrasted the man who saved me from the path of self-destruction with those I'd just observed on my flight. I couldn't picture Doc Hildebrand looking in admiration at the image of the macho man on the screen who kills at will, and drinks, and smokes, and dances, and fornicates. Yet this is the icon of a twenty-first-century man! What does this say about men in general and society as a whole?

Having a ball

The man I saw with a sports magazine was looking at men who are considered heroes because they can kick a ball, catch a ball, hit a ball, run with a ball, throw a ball, and at night have a ball while drinking their highballs. I used to idolize men like that. I thought being great at your sport made people look up to you, made you somebody. I was proud to be a cut above the rest. However, I have come to recognize that these games are based mostly upon three things—deception, pride, and brutality—and these traits don't belong in the heart of a real man. To make matters worse, we, as a society, have linked this package of false manhood with sex appeal.

For instance, the 2004 Super Bowl halftime show featured the now infamous Janet Jackson "wardrobe malfunction," which resulted in her momentary exposure before a general audience. Many in the sports and entertainment media complained about the "inappropriate, offensive, and embarrassing incident," and political leaders and a number of Christians joined the chorus of disapproving voices. However, a number of more thoughtful observers clearly saw the contradiction. *Time* magazine referred to it as "The Hypocrisy Bowl," and several other commentators noted the same double standard. Almost no one protests the scantily clad cheerleaders on the sidelines or the even more minimally clad models in the commercials. Where is the consistency? I am not opposed to recreation when it is wholesome and enjoyable for everyone, but the best I can say for the sports culture today is that it has gotten way off track!

I wondered on the plane that day, *Where are the men with a biblical frame of reference and the courage to stand for principle? Where are the men who say, "It doesn't matter what my upbringing was, God's grace is sufficient for me"? Where are the men who will stand for right in their homes, work places, communities, and churches—not in the power of their flesh, but in the power of Almighty God?* God is calling you and me to be such men, and by His grace we can!

Daniel stood up for principle in his day. He chose a den of hungry lions rather than compromise his conscience. John Bunyan stood up for principle in his day. Imprisoned for preaching the gospel, he would not quit. He picked up his pen and wrote that powerful allegory that has led thousands to find a walk with God—*The Pilgrim's Progress*. Abraham Lincoln stood up for principle in his day. He fearlessly stood against the popular Goliath of slavery—and earned an assassin's bullet.

These were men of courage, integrity, purpose, and heart. We need men like that today—men who will break the bands that enslave them, men who will not shirk their God-given duty to lead and nurture their families, men who will take hold of divine grace to be the patriarchs and priests of their homes after God's likeness.

THE PRESIDENT

When we arrived at our destination, I called the president of the airline. His secretary politely informed me, "Sir, you can't just pick up the phone and call the president of a major airline."

"Yes, I'm sure that is usually true, but I believe that God wants me to talk to him. If you tell him I'm on the phone, I'm sure he'll talk with me."

I was on hold for just a couple of minutes, and the president of the airline picked up the phone. I knew this had to be divine intervention, and I told him, "Sir, I am not calling to complain or yell at you, but I'd like to share my story."

He agreed to listen, so I proceeded to tell him about our family's move to the wilderness to find a real Christian experience; about how it had become an important part of the purpose of my life to raise real men; about how, in order to accomplish that, we had given our sons the best and guarded them from all the rest; and then . . . then I got on his airplane and down comes the screen portraying this counterfeit, and how my sons had to force themselves to ignore the images paraded in front of them, and that for this privilege we had paid almost a thousand dollars each.

There was a quiet pause in our conversation, and then this sharp executive began to speak from his heart.

"Mr. Hohnberger, that's how I was raised. I had almost totally forgotten. Thank you for reminding me. What can I do for you?"

Encouraged by his openness, I pressed on, "Well, we return in three weeks. I know your passengers expect a movie, but could it at least be a family movie?"

"Yes, we could do that, Mr. Hohnberger. I guarantee you there will be a family movie on your flight."

"Sir, it's not that I doubt you, but could I call you the day before our flight and just verify it?"

"Certainly," he replied.

Three weeks later I called his office again, and this time the secretary put me right through. "I have a family movie picked out just for you and your family. You're going to be pleased!"

"Thanks," I said as I hung up.

In spite of his words, a few doubts lingered in my mind. Could one Christian *really* influence the course of an airline? We are often tempted with the old "you can't fight city hall" mentality. We fall into this pattern of thinking in many areas of our lives, accepting the way things are as if they are great, unalterable facts of life. In so doing, we often don't see these seemingly impossible barriers for what they really are—opportunities! I wrestled with these types of thoughts as we took off and the time came for the movie. Would it really happen? Would this man keep his word? Would his crew follow through? Could God actually get the airline to change their plans?

SOMEONE WITH A LOT OF POWER

Suddenly the captain's voice crackled over the intercom, "Ladies and gentlemen, the regularly scheduled movie will not be seen today. In its place we have a special family movie."

You could just feel the wave of groans that passed through that crowd of passengers.

I heard someone ask a flight attendant what was going on. "I don't know exactly," she responded, "but the orders came from the very top. Someone very important—someone with a lot of power—is on board today, and he had it changed."

I smiled to myself because in a sense she was right. My God was with me! In my own way, I had stood in the gap and made up the hedge to protect my family, and in my weakness, the Lord was strong to work an impossible change. One man with God can make a difference!

God is calling us, men. We have a position in our families and society that no one else can fill. Regardless of our past, regardless of our role models or lack thereof, regardless of our age or position, God wants to make us real men—men to "make up the hedge" and "stand in the gap" for our loved ones. Let's not disappoint Him. If we accept the challenge, young women will no longer be complaining about the state of young men because, in our homes, we will have raised a new generation of patriarchs. God wants to write a revised version of Ezekiel 22:30. "I sought for a man among them and I found YOU!"

CHAPTER 1
IN SEARCH OF MEN
Questions to Consider for Personal Inventory or Group Discussion

1. What kind of man would my loved ones say that I am? Patriarch? Playboy? Pansy? Procrastinator? Protector?
2. Have I bought into the false portrait of manhood?
3. Am I insensitive? Uncaring? "Me only"? What would my wife and kids say?
4. What lies has the devil bound me with?
5. In what ways is he taking my children captive through ungodly influences?
6. How is he enticing my wife?
7. What am I beholding? What are my loved ones beholding? In movies? In music? In sports? On the Internet? In magazines?
8. Is my home matriarchal or patriarchal? Is there a proper blend of the masculine and feminine roles?
9. What will be my response to God's call to be a man of principle?
10. Will I reclaim my legacy as a man of power?

A Real
Man

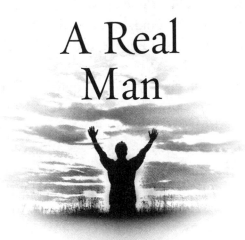

"The Lord has sought for Himself a man after His own heart."
—1 Samuel 13:14, NKJV

Our overseas trip finally ended and we returned home. But my reflections didn't stop. I wondered what it would have been like to see a real man portrayed on that screen. What would he have looked like in flesh and blood?

People were made in the image of God, but how many of us have a clear understanding about what this means? After all, where do we go to get to know, I mean really get to know, the image of God? Originally, God designed that every man, every father, should be a reflection of the divine character of God and that any child would know what God is like because they know what their father is like. Unfortunately, after sin entered the world, this image of God's character became so distorted in most cases that it was useless. To help us out, Jesus became a man so that we might get to know what God is like.

A MAN'S MAN OR A WIMP?

Those men who saw Jesus were never the same again, whether or not they accepted Him as Savior. The devil quickly realized that if Christ's life was portrayed accurately by His followers, many of the false ideas he was cultivating would be lost. So he worked very subtly to get Christians to overemphasize some of Christ's characteristics while ignoring others.

Just think about it. When someone says you should be "Christlike," what picture comes to your mind? Someone who is always gentle, kind, and patient? One who strives to please and avoid confrontation? That's the image I had.

I attended a parochial school where religious instruction was an everyday subject for my contemplation. Most of the art work and images I saw went along with this picture of a very soft man—one with baby-smooth skin and immaculately combed hair and beard, not to mention a boyish body and sensitive features. I am sure the artists had the best intentions. However, the general presentation of Christ was not exactly a man's man.

When I started studying the Bible for myself, I was amazed and excited to realize that the impressions of Jesus that I grew up with were *not* balanced and that Christlikeness does include the firmer virtues. I came to see Him as the real Man that He is—a man's Man—One with muscle and sinew, courage and tenacity, and true independence. Christ was no wimp. He was the model Man. And it is from studying Him and the men who walked intimately with Him that four foundational principles of real manhood have emerged in my thinking and experience—courage, integrity, purpose, and heart. Of course, there is much more to the picture of real manhood than these four qualities; nevertheless, these sketch an outline within which we can pencil the fine details.

PRINCIPLE I: A REAL MAN IS COURAGEOUS

Few men have faced a more difficult choice than Moses did. Raised and trained to become the chief ruler of Egypt at a time when that nation was leading the world, he chose instead to cast his lot with a discouraged, stubborn bunch of slaves. (See Exodus 2 and 3.) That took courage!

It took courage for him to respond to God's call and choose "rather to suffer affliction with the people of God, than to enjoy the pleasures of sin for a season." It took courage to esteem "the reproach of Christ greater riches than the treasures of Egypt."[1] It took courage to lead an

---

1. Hebrews 11:24–26.

undisciplined mob into the wilderness and teach them the ways of God.

Men, God has a calling for every one of us just as He did for Moses. And that calling begins with the people nearest us—our wives and our children. He is calling us to lead our families out of a mediocre existence into a living experience. He wants us to lead as Moses did—under Him. He calls us to command our households in such a manner that they know and love the ways of the Lord.[2]

It takes real courage to respond to that divine calling, but it is foolish not to, because others are eager to command our families after them for less than honorable motivations. The fashion designers are commanding our families, and our families are obeying. The video producers are commanding our families, and our families are obeying. The drug addicts, the music groups, and the false shepherds are commanding our families, and our families are obeying.

For our families' sakes, we must command something—not to control them, but because we care about them. We must expect them to live by moral standards and to follow proper guidelines and rules—to be responsible in the home, to speak respectfully, to dress properly, and to have hairstyles that reflect a holy God. But in order to command it, we must live it. We cannot command what we ourselves do not live.

OLD MAN JOHNSON

I remember our neighbor, Old Man Johnson. This man grew apples that looked as good as the ones in the Garden of Eden must have looked. The problem was that Old Man Johnson loved his apples, and he wouldn't let us have any. One day I saw his car drive away, and I told my friend, "Come on. He's gone. Let's go raid that tree." I didn't know that it was his wife who had driven away.

When he saw us in the tree, Old Man Johnson shouted, and we immediately jumped down, intending to run for our lives! I don't know how it happened, but when I jumped and landed, a hand as strong as an old gnarled oak branch got hold of my collar, and that man paddled my backside—not in anger, but out of principle. And he wasn't yet

---

2. See Genesis 18:19.

done. He marched me over to my house and rang the doorbell. When my dad answered the door he said, "Mr. Hohnberger, I caught your son raiding my apple tree."

My father invited him in and got the whole story. You know what? My dad thanked the man! "Thank you for disciplining my son and bringing him back home, Mr. Johnson. If you ever catch him doing something like that again, feel free to spank him and give him a good turn too!"

As the man disappeared down our walk, I began to really fear what was going to happen to me because, you see, my father was a courageous man, and I knew he wasn't finished with me yet. I thought, *I am in big, big trouble now!* My father gave me the whipping of my life. He gave it to me because I was in the wrong; he gave it to me because he loved me; and he gave it to me because I had to learn the just consequences for ungodly behavior.

Imagine that same situation today. We'd sue Mr. Johnson, take his home, and cut down his apple tree, and little Jimmy Hohnberger would end up in prison because "no one can control the behavior of boys these days." I am not exaggerating this outcome. In our day, the vast majority of the men in prison grew up without a father figure in the home. I was blessed to grow up in a community where neighborhood "patriarchs" were not afraid to discipline little Jimmy Hohnbergers. They did so out of an understanding of right and wrong, of duty and morality. They did so because they had the courage to set godly limits and to enforce them for the sake of those committed to their care.

On the other hand, courage will also lead a man to defend the underdog—as Moses did when he was God's instrument in freeing the Israelite slaves from their Egyptian taskmasters. My father had this type of courage as well.

"I AM HERE FOR YOU!"

In 1964 I entered parochial high school as a fifteen-year-old freshman. It may be hard for those who have seen me speaking before thousands of people to realize that I was not an outgoing child. I was quiet and polite, yet I had a mischievous nature. I enjoyed sports and played football, but I was not a jock, nor did I possess a particularly keen mind. I was an average guy who generally blended in. But for some unknown reason, the history teacher took an intense disliking to me. I dealt with this problem by keeping quiet and avoiding trouble.

One day in class, the teacher was writing on the board while we sat watching in our seats. Suddenly the teacher whipped around and snarled, "Jim Hohnberger, *shut up!*"

Now you must remember that in those days, one didn't question authority. But I had been raised with a high sense of justice, and I politely responded, "I didn't say anything, sir."

His face turned red. "I said, *SHUT UP!*"

"But I never said anything."

In this school, they'd spank you with a size twelve tennis shoe if you got more than two wrong answers on the religion quiz. I knew of another student whose arm had been broken when one of the "brothers" got upset and had thrown him up against the lockers. I realized I might be in for a similar fate when this history teacher, Mr. Frances, came charging toward me, knocked my books off the desk, and grabbed hold of my shirt. He lifted me off the floor and slammed my back against the blackboard and started pounding my head against it. This man was large and tough. He taught history but was also the wrestling coach. I couldn't fight him conventionally because I would lose, and I certainly wasn't going to put up with being unfairly attacked, so I forcibly introduced my knee to a certain portion of his anatomy. He made a startled gasp and collapsed on the floor. I ran for my life—the whole three miles home! By the time I arrived, the principal had called my mother, and my father was on his way home from work.

My father arrived and said, "Jim, just tell the whole truth." So I told him what had happened, that I had taken down a teacher and that the whole school was probably talking about it. "Don't worry," he assured me. "I am going to be by your side all the way through this." He glanced at my head and told me to get in the car. He drove me to see old Doc Hildebrand.

The doctor examined my head and was appalled. "He was assaulted all right," he told my father. "He has a concussion, and there is still a lump on the back of his head the size of a goose egg. This was a straight-out attack, and I will testify in court to the accuracy of my diagnosis. You could kill somebody this way!"

Dad thanked him and concluded, "I don't think it'll come to that. I think we'll get this settled at the school board meeting tonight!"

My dad seemed awfully confident. I was shaking in my boots that evening when we sat down with the school board. I felt very small in a conference room filled with men wearing their priestly robes. Every-thing about them spoke of power and control. As if reading my thoughts, my dad whispered in my ear. "Don't worry. I am here for you."

When the history teacher began to speak, I began to wonder just what my father could do. This teacher stood before the board and lied through his teeth about what had actually happened. When he finished, it was my turn, and I was terrified. I looked at my father and seemed to draw strength from him, and so I straightened my shoulders and spoke to the board quietly and calmly—the exact opposite of how I felt inside. Even my history teacher knew my presentation had the ring of truth to it. He came over to me, got right in my face, and started poking me in the chest, softly at first, but then hard enough to make me stagger, all the while chanting in an excited voice, in time with the pokes—"Liar! Liar! LIAR!"

Just how far this might have continued I have no idea, because my father, quiet and unassuming Henry Hohnberger, rose to his full height, all of five feet eight inches! He may have only weighed 150 pounds, but he grabbed that teacher by the collar and told him to sit down—or else! Then he started to talk. I wish I could remember fully and do justice to his speech, but I was just too terrified.

My father was normally a quiet, very stoic German man, but not on this day. "Gentlemen of the school board," he began, "this situa-tion did not happen because your teacher lost control of his temper, even though we have all seen his temper displayed right before our eyes. This situation occurred because you, Mr. Principal, have allowed the situation to develop. You have even encouraged a situation where your teachers rule by intimidation and brute force. I've been in this town too long not to know about other acts of violence perpetrated by faculty members upon the students. Now one of your teachers has attacked and injured my son. This happens because your leadership is such that teachers have no fear of being disciplined, no fear of any consequences, and while all of you may be men who have given your lives to the priesthood, you certainly haven't given them to God! You, as a board, have an obligation to end this type of behavior, and you don't stop it by reprimanding the teacher. You stop it by removing the person really responsible, and that is the principal. He is the one who sets the tone of the school. Your teachers act as they do because someone has encouraged it. You can finish this problem right here tonight."

I was shocked when he asked for the principal's head, and even more shocked when the man resigned on the spot, admitting it was all true. The school board then decided my father was correct. The teachers had simply acted as they were allowed to act. Instead of firing the history teacher, the board formally disciplined him.

I walked out of that meeting knowing for certain that *my* father was the most courageous man in the world. This was not the Hollywood version of courage but the real thing. It was a lone man standing on his convictions in defense of the defenseless, and it is here, when true courage must be exercised, that a man becomes a *real* man.

COUNTERCULTURE

A man exercises courage when he puts down the toys of childhood and becomes the leader, the patriarch of his home, the priest of the family, the provider and protector for all those under his care. It takes courage because it means choosing to be different from virtually all other men you may know. If men would do this, there would be a mighty revival in our families and in our churches.

True courage is not distinguished primarily by brave feats for the world to see. Real courage is revealed in the hundreds of quiet, consistent actions that make us heroes in the eyes of our wives and our children. It takes courage because you may very well have to blaze your own pathway with no example to follow. It takes courage to spend the evening hours playing with your children while everyone else is working, watching TV, or surfing the Web. It takes courage to make your family the top priority. It takes courage to live day in and day out solely for their benefit. It takes courage to step up in opposition to the expected norms of society and the church.

When God brought me face to face with the fact that I was not a real man in His eyes, I realized I needed to drastically change the program of my life. To make a long story short, Sally and I decided to sell a lucrative business in suburban Wisconsin, abandon the trappings of outward success, and move to a simple log cabin in the wilderness of northwest Montana. We wanted to conduct an all-out experiment to see if Christianity could work for us where it really mattered—in our hearts and in our home. That took courage—more than I had ever had to exercise before.

You've heard of the "counterculture movement." Well, being a real man is the *true* counterculture. Our actions were counter to the views of our friends, our families, and our church. Many people misunderstood not only our actions but also our motives. It takes courage to endure situations like this. Yet the courage to stand alone on my convictions was the legacy my father left me, and it is a legacy I've tried to pass on to my boys. It takes courage to be different—not just for the sake of being different, but for the sake of finding that which society has utterly missed and to which many churches seem blind.

Moses possessed this kind of courage, and he had no regrets. If Moses had chosen to be Pharaoh of Egypt, where would he be now? It's likely he would be a mummy buried beneath a pyramid or displayed in a museum. Moses had the courage to accept his divine calling, and where is he now? He is one of God's all-time greats.

PRINCIPLE 2: A REAL MAN DEVELOPS INTEGRITY

Integrity is simply honesty and uprightness. It is the way you deal with others when no one else would ever know. Many of us were not raised understanding or practicing true integrity.

Neither was Zacchaeus. He was a tax collector who regularly padded his pockets with pilfered profits. No one trusted him—I mean no one! That is, until he met Jesus. You see, Zacchaeus had come under conviction that he wanted to be a real man with genuine integrity. Everyone else laughed at him and gave him a wide berth. But not Jesus! He read the real intent of Zacchaeus's heart and directed him just how to regain his lost integrity.[3] He has done the same for me, and He will do it for you too!

THE HIGH COST OF LOW LIVING

We had been living in the wilderness for a few years and were beginning to understand how Christianity really works when we took an opportunity to go back to Appleton, Wisconsin, and visit our parents. While we were there, the Lord impressed me that I needed to deal with something from my past. Right away I felt resistance rise in my heart. "Lord, I don't want to do that. That was years ago. I'll be embarrassed to death." I knew I should take care of it, but much to my dismay, God wasn't through with me yet. He said, *"And Jim, I want you to take your boys along."*

My boys were ten and eight years old at the time, and God made it clear they could gain a lesson in being real men from my experience. I didn't have the heart to tell them or my wife what I was going to do; I just asked them to come with me to a store because there was something I wanted them to see. We drove to H. C. Pranges & Company, the large department store in my hometown. All the way there I fought the urge to turn around and forget the whole idea, but when I arrived at the store, the very first parking spot outside the door was available. It was as if the Lord had arranged everything to be as easy as possible for me, so I wouldn't change my mind.

Before getting out of the car I told my boys, "Don't ask any questions or say anything. You are about to witness the high cost of low living. When we return to the car you can ask any questions you want." They didn't have a clue what was up. Sally was puzzled also, but she was content to let me play out whatever was in my heart.

We soon found ourselves seated in front of the manager, a woman who was used to complaints and problems, and there was an air of apprehension and tension in the room. She attempted a smile and politely asked, "And what can I do for you today, Mister . . ."

"Hohnberger," I interjected.

---

3. See Luke 19:1–10.

"Uh, yes, Mister Hohnberger?"

"Ma'am, when I was fourteen years old I stole a sweater from your store. You see, there was a girl I wanted to impress, and I didn't have the money to buy it. I knew it was wrong, but I did it anyway. I've become a Christian since then, and God has asked me to make it right. Here is a check to pay for the sweater."

She glanced at the check and said, "Mister Hohnberger, sweaters didn't cost this much in 1963 . . . don't even cost this much today!"

"You're right, but your store has been deprived of the interest the money from that sweater would have earned all these years."

"Well, we won't prosecute you."

Prosecute me! I had never thought of that! But if she noticed my open mouth she didn't act like it, because she continued, "I don't know what to say. I've been in retail for thirty years, and no one has ever done what you are doing. I am not a Christian myself, but I commend you for your integrity in making past wrongs right."

When we returned to our car, my boys were dumbstruck. They had never thought their father would do anything like that. I explained, "Boys, I have found Jesus, and He is calling me to a life of integrity. You have a chance to start your lives with a relatively clean slate, but I have to clear up the past. God's ideal for us is to have 'a conscience void of offence toward God, and toward man,' like it says in Acts 24:16. You just witnessed the high cost of low living. Don't ever compromise yourselves like I did. It's not worth it."

I used to think that integrity was something we were born with, but this is not the case. Integrity is developed through a lifetime of choices and is more costly to obtain and keep than houses, lands, or any of the toys we men are attracted to. Praise God that no matter how many times we have failed, we can go back and, in Christ, regain the integrity God designed we should have.

PICK UP THE BALL

After the experience in the department store, I drove back to my parents' home. My thoughts drifted back to another day when I was fifteen. It was springtime and my family was at supper, which in our home was a time of camaraderie as we shared the day's events. As the conversation drifted from one topic to another, it eventually turned to the humidifier that had been installed the previous fall to compensate for the dehydrating effects of artificial heat. My mother commented, "That humidifier was such a blessing this last winter."

My father looked up from his plate and inquired, "Bernice, did they ever bill us for that humidifier?"

"Now that you mention it, I don't think they ever did."

"That was six months ago; they must have forgotten."

"Looks like we got us a free humidifier," I sang out. I was still struggling with my own ideas of right and wrong. I had stolen that sweater the year before, and now a free humidifier seemed like a stroke of luck—at least until I saw the look of disappointment on my father's face. He said nothing as he rose from the table, looked up a phone number and dialed.

"This is Henry Hohnberger. You installed a humidifier for us last fall, but I don't think you ever billed us . . . yes, that's right . . . correct. That's the address. What's that—the service department never turned in the work order? Well, I can assure you it was completed. . . . Yes, that would be fine. I'll send you a check tomorrow."

As he sat back down at the table, I will never forget his words. "Jimmy, you never get ahead at someone else's expense. You never overreach. You need to know when life is over that you've treated all men honestly. If you don't know this, you are only half a man."

My father gave me a legacy. If all of us were measured by that standard, how would we rate—a half a man, a quarter of a man, or no man at all? We have all failed in our dealings with others; we have all dropped the ball. But in Christ we can pick it back up and become true men of integrity.

Principle 3: A real man lives a life of PURPOSE

If ever there was a story in the Bible of purpose apparently thwarted and yet genuinely fulfilled, it has to be that of Joseph! Imagine being at once the favorite son and hated brother, and then suddenly finding yourself Potiphar's slave. Some life—not much purpose there anymore. His father had been grooming him to lead the family, but those plans were shattered. How would all those dreams God had given him ever be fulfilled now? Joseph had a choice: He could become bitter or he could trust.

Joseph chose to trust God in the midst of these devastating circumstances. Thus, he did his best at whatever work lay nearest. This is the secret that gave purpose to Joseph's life no matter where he was—Jacob's tent, Potiphar's house, the royal dungeon, or Pharaoh's palace. Day by day, hour by hour, Joseph did his best at whatever work was nearest to him, believing that God controlled his life and had placed that work there for him to do, content to leave the ultimate working of the purpose of his life with God. And because of Joseph's attitude, God used slavery and imprisonment as a school to prepare him to become prime minister of Egypt!

How many of us would choose that training program? I dare say none of us would—but when Joseph reflected on it afterwards he could say that while others meant it to him for evil, God meant it to him for good.

SANDBOX

The outset of this type of life is scary, because it means trusting your life, your future, and everything you have in Someone Else's hands when you don't know how things are going to turn out. Yikes! It means that Someone Else controls your destiny! That feels frightening until you find that the Someone Else is more trustworthy than you are, that His purpose for your life is broader than you could ever dream, and that He has the uncanny ability to make even the worst of events turn out for your best.

When Sally and I discovered this, it became the great theme of our lives, but it didn't happen overnight. You see, at one time my life was caught up in pursuing myths. These myths are the devil's counterfeits for real purpose. Almost everyone has some kind of purpose, but most people are pursuing a mirage, a myth that leads you on and on, ever receding before you. God began to show me that, like Joseph, I would find my real purpose in life when I trusted Him and sought to faithfully perform the work nearest me.

For me that meant reclaiming my role as the leader of my family. It meant learning to be a servant to my wife's real needs and supplier of my sons' deeper desires. That was a lot harder than simply providing for them financially as I had always done. It meant learning to control my words when speaking to my wife. It meant becoming a playmate for my boys, and I'll admit I didn't always like it. I was a businessman used to making deals and turning a profit. Now I found myself questioning just exactly what purpose I was accomplishing as I sat in the sandbox playing "truckie" with my boys. I remember questioning God at the time, *Is this really what You called me from my important pursuits to do?*

God reminded me of Joseph and how his high expectations had seemingly been buried beneath the rough, the ordinary, and the pointless. *"Jim,"* He said to me that day, *"this is the work I have set nearest you right now. Will you faithfully perform it and trust your future with Me?"*

So I sat in the sandbox and played, and eventually I saw God's purpose. You see, I am a stubborn German by birth. At the time I didn't realize how much "Hitler" was in me. God could see it, though, and He was putting me through a training program calculated to subdue the "Hitler" and cultivate a "Luther." It was a good program. As God allowed me to face my own self-centeredness again and again and again, I began to see He had a better way than I had ever thought of. Under His guidance, I gained the hearts of my sons, and I still have them today even though they are in their late twenties. My wife is still the love of my life, and our marriage is strong and fulfilling. At the time I had no idea that we would one day be running a ministry that touched people around the world, but our ministry today is a direct outgrowth of learning to walk with God, to revitalize our marriage, and to reconnect our family—my time in the sandbox.

If you catch this vision, if you are willing to seek the *depth* of God's purpose where you are presently and trust your future with Him, then God can develop the *breadth* of where He is taking you. And you will find greater satisfaction and more real adventure than you could ever have invented on your own.

We find the real purpose of manhood when we learn to "cease . . . from man, whose breath is in his nostrils: for wherein is he to be accounted of?"[4] This means more than avoiding the temptation to follow

---

4. Isaiah 2:22.

other men. It means you cannot trust in your own intellect and wisdom. If you are to truly trust God, you cannot write your own script of where you want to be and what you want to do and how you want everything to happen. God doesn't work things out the way we do. He loves the unusual, the strange twists in the plots, and the miraculous surprise endings that leave us shaking our heads with awe and wonder at His perfect planning, so that even the evil done to us by others is turned about to work for our benefit.

I have found that to truly live a life of purpose, I don't have to be in charge. I have to come to know and trust the One who is in charge. It is liberating to know that what comes into my life today comes because God allows and plans for it. I can't describe the peace that comes from knowing that what God places before me this day is His will for me and I am to do my best at it no matter how great or how trivial.

PRINCIPLE 4: A REAL MAN HAS HEART

The temple at Jerusalem should have been the most sacred place on earth, a place where people could come to learn about God, to understand His working in their lives, and to worship Him. But in Jesus' day its original purpose had been lost, and it had turned into something that resembled a noisy cattle market. Loud voices bargaining over the price of animals for sacrifice competed with the chink of coins. Cows mooed. Sheep baaed. Doves cooed. It was a mess! And no one seemed to have the courage or integrity to do anything about it. No one, that is, until Jesus showed up on the scene.

Just picture Him, if you will. He was in the prime of manhood—a tanned, muscular, skilled craftsman, just beginning His public mission. He entered upon the temple scene unrecognized and unknown, a simple man from an obscure town. As far as the "big guys" were concerned, He was just a country bumpkin. He had no credentials, no degrees, no office, and no authority, at least to all appearances.

But Jesus was a real man, a man's Man. His eye took in the whole scene—the money changers and the livestock salesmen turning a profit on the love of God; the cold-hearted priests boasting of their superior religion while totally lacking compassion for hurting people; and outward forms of worship carried out to the "t" without real understanding. He saw that something must be done and that God was calling Him to do it.

So He stood up and commanded, "Take these things away; make not My Father's house a house of merchandise."[5] In case they misunderstood Him, He picked up a whip and drove them out. He knocked over their tables and sent the money rolling across the marble pavement. None dared to question His authority. They all fled—officers, priests, brokers, and cattle traders with all their animals. Finally, the temple was quiet and peaceful. Those that remained—the honest in heart—crowded around Jesus as He ministered to them.

The offenders finally stopped running and began to wonder why they had allowed a "nobody" to chase them out. Slipping back to the temple, they see Jesus doing the very work that they should have done. Sadly, though, instead of humbly recognizing the good being accomplished and picking up their real work, they became Jesus' bitterest enemies. They made life as difficult for Him as possible and tried in every way to discredit Him. They even plotted His death.

Three and a half years later, Jesus stands on the Mount of Olives overlooking the temple. He is surrounded by a vast crowd of supporters, and popular opinion is in His favor. In fact, the populace is pushing to crown Him King. Now He could really put His critics in their place—and their greatest fear is that He will do just that. Instead, He weeps—not just a few silent tears, in my opinion, but heart-wrenching sobs. The wondering crowd doesn't understand. This is a day of rejoicing! Why is He weeping?

How could He explain to them the deep longing in His soul to cleanse not only the temple in Jerusalem, but also the temple in the hearts of His people? How could they understand the anguish He feels at their stubborn refusal of the only remedy that would save them from their fatal condition? How could He make them see that their hour of mercy was nearly ended? How could He let them go?

You see, Jesus had the courage, the integrity, and the God-directed purpose to take on the temple scene. He was firm, unvarying, unflinching

---

5. John 2:16.

to carry out His duty. But oh, what heart He possessed for the people. What deep compassion He felt for them. How tenderly He treated the honest in heart. How longingly He pleaded with the stubborn.

Real men have heart. They feel for the deeper needs of others. They cry. Jesus not only cried for His people, but He cried for His good friend Lazarus. Real men *do* have feelings, are *not* afraid to express them, and *don't worry* if others see them being vulnerable.

A NIGHT OF TEARS

I'll never forget the time I cried all night. My father was dying of emphysema. He had smoked Lucky Strikes from his teens onward, and now he was dependant upon oxygen twenty-four hours a day. I was home for a visit and found him in very bad shape. My father understood his condition and asked all of us to respect his wishes not to be placed on any life-prolonging equipment.

The day I flew back to Montana, my brother called to tell me that they had found Dad unconscious on the floor that morning. They called the ambulance, emergency protocol took over, and my father ended up in ICU on a ventilator. The doctor approached my family with my father's poor prognosis and presented them with the options. My brother wanted my input.

I had to make a decision—one of the hardest decisions of my life. On the one hand, I wanted to honor my father's wish and let him die in peace. On the other, I had just spent days with him—the man who'd spanked me for stealing apples, the man who'd stood by my side before the school board, the man who in his simple, nonflashy way had provided me a significant part of the precious legacy of what it is like to be a real man—and I knew in my heart of hearts that my father wasn't ready to die. This isn't to say I could read his heart, only that in the understanding I had of my father, he hadn't yet made his peace with God. My brother awaited my decision, and, ready or not, I had promised along with the rest of my siblings to honor his wish that he be allowed to die, as he had put it, "with respect, honor, and dignity."

My heart screamed "No!" while my mind demanded a "Yes!" I mumbled something to my brother about honoring my father's wishes and letting him go. It was eight o'clock in the evening, and I went off by myself and poured my heart out to God about my dad, pleading for more time for him, a little more grace that he might be prepared. It was the first night I ever spent in crying and praying. Unashamedly, tears rolled down my cheeks as I considered what I was losing and what he was losing. Finally, in the early morning hours, the Lord impressed me to stop my crying and pleading and write Dad's eulogy.

EULOGY?

I was stunned. I had been praying for God to spare my dad's life a little longer, and I was being told to write his eulogy? I couldn't; I wouldn't; my feelings rebelled against this acknowledgment of his death. My mind was certain of God's direction, and still I questioned it. *Are You sure, Lord?* I asked reluctantly.

"Have courage, Jim. I will give you the words."

I got a yellow legal pad and sat down at two in the morning, my heart in my throat, to write the final words I would say at Dad's funeral:

> It's not easy letting go of your father. After all, I am bone of his bone, flesh of his flesh, and what do you say after he is gone? Dad was not a great athlete or coach, not a great businessman or entrepreneur, not a rocket scientist or great speaker. Dad was not great in the eyes of the world, but he was great in my eyes.
>
> No movies will be made of his life, and no books written of his accomplishments, but he was unique in his own sort of way. Dad was dependable. You could always trust what he said. You could rest with confidence that he'd be on time. He remained a loyal husband and a responsible father. He was simple and never tried to impress anyone. He got along with one car, a nice home, and a wife who never had to work outside the home. He was neat and tidy. All things had their place, and he made sure they were in it. He taught us to respect others, to work hard, and to carry our own responsibilities in life.
>
> Growing up, we could count on him to stand with us if wrongly accused and to stand firmly on the side of right when we were wrong. He gave us the basics so missing in today's

society—namely a solid home environment. We ate our meals as a family. We had a clear sense of right and wrong. We had good morals. And we had his example of living within your means and paying your bills on time.

In short, Dad gave us what he had, and these things have helped all of us stay married and have good marriages. He gave us the basics, and they are the basics I will pass on to my own children and their children. Dad was truly a simple man and yet his simplicity had a profound effect upon my life. Thanks, Dad, for the building blocks of life. Thanks for being you. There is no other dad in the world I would want. God knew what I needed, and that is why He gave me you!

By the time I had written the last word, the page was smeared and wrinkled with tears, but I knew in my mind what my heart had always known, and that is what a special man he was to me.

It was still early morning the next day when my family called. I knew what the news would be, so I steadied myself as I took the phone. Sorrow gave way to incredible joy as I heard, "They're not just taking Dad out of the ICU, but out of the hospital and transferring him to a nursing home. The doctor just told us, 'He does better off life support than on it!' "

I was thrilled! God *had* heard my prayers, and He *had* answered. However, I also knew that Father was a very sick man and the end could come any time. We were scheduled to fly overseas on ministry-related business for the next three weeks! Would he last until I came home? On the airplane, God impressed me to write my father a very personal letter and share my experience the night I had written his eulogy. I was to tell him all that God had put in my heart, all my love and all my concerns. I was to send it to him as soon as we landed and to include a copy of the eulogy I had written that awful night he was reportedly dying.

Lord, I prayed, *I can't do that. It is just too personal. I mean, no one sends someone his or her own eulogy. It might be misunderstood—as if I am anxious for his death.* But even as I thought of these excuses, I knew God was speaking straight to my heart and mind, so I wrote the letter on the plane, and as soon as we touched down I sent the package.

Then I worried about my father's response. Five days later, my mother called. She had taken my letter to Father and he had told her, "Thank Jim, for he truly understands! Tell him his letter touched me in a way that nothing else could have."

The day we were flying home, my father died. Two days later, I was able to deliver that eulogy at his funeral, not just in grief, but in the joy of knowing that God had touched my father in a special way and that in his own simple way my dad had responded. My long night of tears was worth it!

Contrary to popular opinion, big boys do cry. They cry over their marriages. They cry over their children. They cry over their churches. They cry for their society. They cry for their family. They cry for their friends and they cry for their enemies—for these are men of courage. These are men of integrity and purpose. These are men of heart.

CHAPTER 2
A REAL MAN

Questions to Consider for Personal Inventory or Group Discussion

1. In what ways has my understanding of the image of God been distorted by society and/or my upbringing?
2. What is my picture of Jesus—a man's man or wimp?
3. Do I command my family because I care for them or to get my way?
4. Do I have the courage to get involved with the real needs of my family?
5. Have I compromised my integrity?
6. What is God asking me to do to reclaim my integrity?
7. What is my purpose in life?
8. Is my purpose self-determined or truly God-directed?
9. Do I feel for the real needs of others? Especially those nearest me?
10. Do they know it? Would my loved ones say I have real heart?
11. Will I begin cooperating with God to become a real man?

The Myth

I have seen all the works that are done under the sun; and indeed,
all is vanity and grasping for the wind.
—*Ecclesiastes 1:14, NKJV*

Robert evaded my questions time after time, making me wonder why he'd asked to counsel with me. At last I blurted out, "Robert, you've got to tell me what is on your mind. I can't help you if you won't share with me."

"Well it's . . . er . . . sort of . . . personal like . . . and I am not sure you'd understand."

"If you'd rather not share, that's fine. We don't need to waste our time sparring for no reason."

"Do men ever talk to you about sex?" he asked bluntly, as if the possible ending of our conversation had at last lit a fire under him.

"It is one of the most common subjects they want to address."

He seemed to visibly relax and then began. "I was raised in a conservative church, and I always feared that I was going to get stuck with a sexually repressed woman from the same environment, and I swore I'd never marry someone without being sure they'd be able to perform.

"I met Susan our junior year at college, and we were intimate before we knew it. We had a good relationship in many ways, and physically she was the most willing, wonderfully adventurous, and eager woman I had ever known. The funny thing was that she was from exactly the type of background I always said I'd never marry a girl from, but the laugh was on me. After graduation we married, and I expected we would have our struggles . . . every couple does, but I never thought physical intimacy would become an issue. However, shortly after the honeymoon she changed. Now we just fight about it constantly."

Robert was chasing a myth—the myth of the perfect sexual partner. He believed that if Susan would only perform to his expectations, he would be happy and fulfilled. I have met countless men who believe Robert's myth. They fantasize that partnering with a woman who has a more voluptuous figure, silkier hair, fuller lips, and a drive to match their own will satisfy them. This ideal woman lives only in their imagination.

The pornography industry makes big bucks off this myth, and in the process they perpetuate it. My father was a photo engraver for a company that contracted with a variety of magazines. When I was a young married man, my father approached me with a dilemma he was wrestling with. His company had accepted a contract with a prominent "girlie" magazine, and my father had been asked to do the photo engraving. He was given indecent shots of young women and asked to touch up the prints so that their anatomy appeared perfectly symmetrical, with unblemished skin and no unsightly marks or unwanted rolls. My father recognized the destructive myth that was being perpetuated and declined to continue applying his skills to such a project—at the peril of losing his job! My point is, though, that no flesh and blood woman—not even the one depicted in print herself—could live up to the myth conjured in the minds of men by these portrayals. Sadly, many men never see through this. They keep pursuing and pursuing, leaving a trail of brokenness behind them and missing the entire purpose for their existence.

But there are other myths men chase.

FUTURE WANTS—THE PURSUIT OF MANKIND

Some time ago, I received a call from a man I had known casually in business. Charles was calling because his wife was giving him "all kinds of grief" about a new business opportunity. He was a successful salesman who made a good income. He and his wife, Pam, were raising two daughters, now of high school age. I wondered what had ruffled their feathers, but I didn't have long to wait.

"Jim, I've had this fantastic offer to head the Mideast sales force. The guy who's retiring was making a fortune."

"What does Pam think about this?"

"She's one hundred percent opposed, and that's the problem."

"Why? Does she object to moving east?"

"Jim, she couldn't come with me. It's not Mideast like 'East Coast.' It's Mideast like Middle East—you know, Lebanon, Syria, Iraq, Kuwait—the whole area, even Iran."

"Well, that certainly puts a different spin on things. Why are you so excited about the idea? Sounds like a good way to become a target."

"Jim, you don't understand. This is not a little raise. I'm looking at bringing in at least another five hundred thousand dollars a year, and probably a lot more."

I could see where this was going. He was star-struck by dollar signs, seeing only a bright financial future, while his wife was worried about the well-being of their family if they separated. "Charles, do you and Pam *need* more money?"

"Well, Jim, you can never have too much money. There's no such thing as too much money."

"You know what I mean, Charles. Are you in trouble financially?"

"No. We've been very lucky, Jim. My income and our investments have made us quite comfortable, but this job is our ticket to the big leagues. I've got to find some way to make her agree before it's too late."

Charles, too, was chasing a myth, the myth that money can buy happiness and security. He had bought into the devil's food cake. Do you know what devil's food cake is? It is something pleasing to the eye that tastes sweet at the time, but which works to destroy our health and happiness. You know how it came to be called devil's food cake? It seems that the cake was so good, the rumor began that the person who'd created it had sold their soul to the devil to get the recipe, and true or not, it is illustrative of the way the devil deals with us. He offers us things that seem so good and never lets on that the price will be our own destruction. Charles believed this deception and thought that happiness would come from something *he had yet to acquire.*

MINISTRY MYTHS

Ray pursued a myth of yet a different variety, but one that is very common. Ray was one of the most dynamic people I have ever met. He'd been a successful businessman before he got tired of making money and sought deeper meaning in religion. His life appeared transformed. Frustrated with the church's slow progress and traditional approach, he had used his business experience to start a television ministry on the local television station and built it into a nationwide ministry. Yet when I met with him, there were large warning signs that all was not well. Ray is a classic example of the occasional hearty soul who avoids the trap of seeking worldly gain and buys the idea that they can find fulfillment in ministry.

MYRIADS OF MYTHS

Then there are those entrapped in seemingly impossible human problems. Lloyd faced such a situation. He was married to a woman who was just plain unpleasant. I met them both and found he wasn't exaggerating the situation at all. She was harsh and demanding and used to getting her own way all of the time. She had bought into the myth that "my way now" was her ticket to happiness, but it was obvious to everyone except her that she was never satisfied. The myth Lloyd understandably pursued was that his wife needed to become an amiable person in order for him to find rest.

The pursuit of myths abounds wherever you turn. Some think that a hobby such as ham radio will satisfy them. Others are enthralled with their sports—golf, tennis, football, racquetball, and more. I've met men captivated by fitness programs, led on by the vague idea that possessing a chiseled, lean body will bring them fulfillment. Other men collect stuff—from the latest tool to model trains or antique cars.

Some men are dissatisfied with where they live. "If only I could live in Hawaii . . . or the Bahamas . . . or Switzerland . . . or the Rocky Mountains, I'm sure life would be more satisfying."

Closely related to this myth is the pursuit of pleasure. SCUBA diving in the Caribbean or surfing the shore of Hawaii may not be things you would choose to find fulfillment, but at one time in my life I thought that if I could only do this or only do that, I would find the happiness I desired. I have met countless men who have a dream, be it climbing the tallest mountains or exploring the unknown. Others are attracted to a life of ease—of wine, women, and song.

I want to remind you of Adam and Eve in the Garden of Eden. God had placed everything needed for their happiness there. Unlike you and me, they did live in a perfect environment. They had access to the tree of life, perfect health, and energy and vitality. They had the perfect occupation, keeping and dressing the Garden—a job uniquely suited to their personalities and challenging to their intellect. On top of all that they were married to the perfect mate.

Can you imagine having the perfect everything and yet thinking there was more for you to obtain? Our first parents did! The devil came to them with a myth, and like most myths it contains a portion of truth. "In the day ye eat thereof, then your eyes shall be opened, and ye shall be as gods."[1] The devil sold them on the idea that there was something more that they needed to make them happy.

I have made my living in sales, and I want to assure you right now that the devil is quite a salesman. Adam and Even bought his story and his myth, and every one of us has inherited this same weakness. Consequently, almost all are convinced that they will find happiness and satisfaction in something they do not now possess. And they are correct. The problem is that what they are pursuing will not deliver that which they seek.

The lives of Elvis Presley, Marilyn Monroe, Howard Hughes, and many others testify to the fact that money, prestige, and popularity do not satisfy. While attaining what many strive for, they found nothingness. Their lives all ended tragically.

---

1. Genesis 3:5.

MY MYTHS

These stories are so familiar to me because in my own life I have pursued the myths as much as anyone else. After all these years, through the grace of God, I can at last see them clearly, and I think when you see them in my life, you will recognize them in your own. So, drift back with me through my memories as I share with you my myths.

My story begins simply. Much of what I learned that had any real value was gleaned growing up in Appleton, Wisconsin. And yet my family, my friends, my teachers, in fact, my whole community, unwittingly taught me a myth that haunted my life for years. It is known as the American Dream. Of course, like most myths, the American Dream incorporates much that is worthy—a good work ethic, an enthusiasm for self-improvement, and a purpose to provide the very best for your family. My family embraced this, and all my training was geared toward helping me internalize this dream. They encouraged me to set and strive for goals early in life.

To this day, I can still remember my first foray into this template of working hard to achieve a goal. I had been doing odd jobs here and there as I grew up, but when my brother was ready to quit his paper route, I got lucky. Then again, perhaps it wasn't luck. My whole family was trained with my parents' work ethic, and the *Appleton Post Crescent* liked my brother's work so much that they gave me the job even though I was officially too young. This first real job provided me contact with other people, and soon I had other odd jobs in addition.

I saved my pennies because I had already set a large goal for myself. I wanted a bike! Not just *any* bike. No. That would never do. I wanted a new Schwinn Western Flyer. It had the very latest in bike technology—double chrome fenders, a horn, and even a light. With front and back carriers, it would be the best bike in the neighborhood. On top of all this, it had something brand new that no other bikes had—gears, three of them! Of course, everyone would notice the bike because it was brilliant red, and the light reflecting off the shiny metal was so bright, it could hurt your eyes.

There was only one small problem. It cost seventy-five dollars, which, when I was twelve, was a lot more money than it is today. I don't know exactly how to account for inflation over the years, but I do know that the company that used to make it for Schwinn sells the exact same bike as a replica, and the price is nearly one thousand dollars as of the time of this writing. Any way you look at it, seventy-five dollars then or one thousand dollars now, it was and still is a lot of money for a twelve-year-old.

Do you know how many papers you have to deliver to earn seventy-five dollars? As hard as it is to believe, I wasn't discouraged. This was what I had been raised to believe in—fulfilling the American Dream. I worked and worked. And I will never, and I mean never, forget the joy of trading seventy-five dollars for that piece of painted metal and polished chrome, nor can I forget my pride at taking it out for that first ride. At that moment, I knew happiness that, I was certain, would never fade away.

But it did begin to fade, and before long it was just a bike, and my thoughts turned to another goal. My first motorized vehicle! I wish you could have seen it—a 1966 Suzuki motorcycle with a 150cc engine. It made all the hours I'd worked at the gas station worthwhile when I rode up to Sally's for a date. Soon we'd be off to the state park or the quarry, with me reveling in the manly roar of the engine and the rush of the wind in our hair. We'd go to dances on the weekends. These were the happy days of rock-and-roll, and we danced the evenings away to a mix of old and new music, doing the limbo, the twist, and the jerk. School mornings would find me and another motorcycle buddy waiting at the corner of Oneida and Ramlen Court for Sally to drive by. With obvious pride, we would escort her to school. I was in my element, and no one could have ridden higher in the saddle.

But soon the excitement became mundane, and my eyes were set on something else that was necessary to complete my satisfaction.

By working full time before entering school and between twenty and forty hours a week during semesters, I managed to obtain the ultimate machine for a young man—a 1960 black Chevy Impala with big fins on the back. And in Sally I had the ultimate hood decoration! What more could anyone wish for? Well . . . there was this one thing.

My mother had instilled in me a reverence for education—not just any education, but a college education! I didn't seek this dream so much for self-improvement but as a way to be seen by others as important, educated, and of course, well-paid. If you're as old as I am, I don't need to remind you of annual salaries in the early 1970s; if you're not, let me explain that the average income when I graduated from college was around eight thousand dollars a year. I set my career goal of earning thirty-thousand dollars a year before I retired. I knew that anyone who made that kind of money was well off. Incredible!

Sally and I got married, and after a rough start in sales, I began making more money than I ever dreamed about. Yet money, in and of itself, while thrilling, was not satisfying. We decided that happiness and fulfillment would come from the things money could buy us. We traded our little starter home for a custom-designed home built just for us. We incorporated all the trendy designs of the 1970s—the sunken living room, a cozy fireplace with built-in bookshelves on each side—and on it went. It was a lovely home. Sally had a station wagon in the driveway, and I had moved on to a Monte Carlo with a Landau roof. We had what seemed a great marriage by many standards, an income most people only dreamed about, and a lovely, custom-built home; yet we were still painfully dissatisfied. In our discussions we sought solutions, set new goals, and dreamed new dreams.

"Sally, I don't like working for someone else. They never want to pay you what you are really worth, and you never have control over your schedule or life. If we owned our own business, I could work when I wanted. We could build something of real value and gain control over our time."

"Jim," Sally responded, "I've never liked the stress you bring home from your current position. I would welcome anything that would give you more control over your work. Let's do it!"

We did start our own business, and it grew into a successful, thriving enterprise. But I soon found that I didn't run my business. It ran me! Being sole proprietor did indeed provide me with all the rewards, but it also gave me all the headaches, from taxes to employee problems. Every month I made more, but I also worked harder! The tasks that only the owner—gulp, that's me—could do seemed to multiply exponentially.

We should have been happy and fulfilled, but both of us sensed there was more to life than what we were achieving. "All work and no play makes Jim a dull boy," Sally reminded me. I knew she was right, and early on in our professional life we began to go out with friends. A typical Friday evening went something like this: We would head out to a Friday evening fish fry sponsored by the Knights of Columbus. I enjoyed these social events, talking with friends I'd known, in some cases, since childhood. We talked and gossiped, washing down fish and chips with cans of beer. It was a great way to begin a summer evening, but we weren't ready to go home yet—we were just getting started! After the fish fry we'd go dancing until midnight. While society was changing its tastes and disco was just becoming popular with those crazy mirrored balls reflecting light everywhere, we still danced the way we always had. I loved the slow dances where you could cuddle up close on the dark dance floor. One of my favorite slow dances was to "Moon River" by Andy Williams. It summed up all our hopes and dreams as we floated in each other's arms and the music carried us away in our thoughts.

It was so romantic to think that Sally and I were indeed off on a grand adventure seeking all life had to offer us. My whole life had been a preparation for the days I was now living in. I was in the fullness of manhood and really felt I had arrived. In Sally I had a beautiful partner; in my business the future seemed unlimited; and socially, as the old commercial said, I was out to "grab all the gusto." So on nights like this, we'd continue to drink and dance. Some of my friends went for fancy drinks, but I was a beer man. An ice-cold Budweiser or maybe a Michelob, which I considered at the time to be the champagne of bottled beers, was just the thing to quench one's thirst. After the dance, Sally and I would accompany friends to a late-night pizza joint, where we would have a large pizza and of course a pitcher or two of beer. By the time we got home, it was usually between one and two in the morning.

I had consumed, if it was an average weekend, something on the order of twelve to fifteen beers and often wasn't feeling so great. I'd flop into bed and the bed would begin rotating—slowly at first but picking up speed, spinning faster and faster, like a merry-go-round in a playground. I don't know if you can relate to this, but you will doubtless understand what happens in your body if you allow the spinning to continue. When the bed first begins to move you've got to stop it—fast—so you quickly place your foot out of the bed on the floor to keep the bed from spinning. Logical, right?

Well, maybe not, because sometimes, in spite of the foot on the floor, I got a certain feeling that tells even someone who has consumed vast quantities of adult beverages that they need to stagger down the hall and put their face in a certain location and soon! I hate to admit it now, but on more than one occasion Sally found me in the morning still firmly gripping the sides of the toilet bowl, sound asleep. Hung over, we would call our friends, who in our shared misery would agree that we'd had a great time! Then we'd make plans to do it again. This was all we knew of having a good time, and it was all our friends knew. You weren't a man if you didn't drink, and getting drunk was how *real* men had a good time. It was expected and even honored to a degree by the world about us.

When I wasn't in the middle of having a "good time," I realized that there wasn't so much that was "good" in the time I spent that way. I was beginning to be dissatisfied with my recreation. Yet this lifestyle was so common, widespread, and universal. What else was there? I had no idea that the entire philosophy bred into me from childhood was faulty, that my whole concept of manhood and masculinity was based on false perceptions intentionally cultivated by the enemy of my soul for my destruction.

My whole focus of life had been upon satisfying some future want. Remember when I graduated from college and thought if I could just make thirty thousand dollars, I would be satisfied? I was soon earning a six-figure income, and I found that when you make a hundred thousand a year, you set your sights on a quarter million, and when you make that, then half a million a year becomes your goal. When you have a small home, you think a larger home will satisfy. Finally, we had a huge log home on forty acres with a private pond, yet we were still not satisfied or happy. I began to think that a second vacation home and a new Corvette would satisfy me.

A pivotal point

I don't know how long I would have continued like this if God had not broken through to my consciousness and woken me up. He used the worst fight Sally and I ever had to open my eyes to the fact that all I was pursuing was vanity. Suddenly, the unpleasant picture of reality forced itself before my reluctant and bewildered eyes. I realized that my character was superficial, my marriage was stale, and I didn't know my own children. Even the biblical truths I had recently embraced and the lifestyle changes I had adopted were not reaching the core of Jim Hohnberger. I had to admit I was empty.

This moment proved to be the great pivotal point of my life. Christ offered to redirect my life. He invited me, as He did that rich young ruler so long ago, to literally sell all that I had and come follow Him. He called me to move to a tiny mountain cabin in northwestern Montana—not for the purpose of hiding or even of finding the perfect location. He gave me the individualized prescription that I needed to find *Him*—not one of the many substitutes for Him—but *Him Himself*. He bid me follow *Him*—not a creed, not a lifestyle, not a set of forms or injunctions. He offered to me *Himself* and in *Him* I found the kernel I had been searching for amidst the chaff of all the myths. In *Him* I found completeness, present satisfaction, and the inward happiness I had tried to find everywhere else. I discovered the reality that "ye are complete in *Him*"![2] When I decided to relinquish control over my life and my future and let God take the reins, I found just what I had been searching for in all the wrong places.

God reordered my priorities and pointed me to my real treasures. He taught me to make relationships first. In Him, I learned to make my wife a priority, not my business. In Him, I learned to make my Matthew and my Andrew a priority, not my selfish interests, not my sports, my news, my TV, or my recreation. In Him I learned to make my character development a priority.

At the time, it felt backwards from all I had been raised for. But I can testify to you today that I have found the real, the genuine, the lasting satisfaction, and no natural disaster or economic depression can rob me

---

2. Colossians 2:10.

of it. I am experiencing that the God of the universe is capable of meeting my deepest needs—even in the most trying circumstances. He is teaching me how to relate to my wife so that our marriage sparkles with the luster of fresh love. He has helped me raise two sons who have grown into real men and have picked up in their youth what took me many years to grasp. While I certainly have not "arrived" in my character development, I am finding true wealth—because God is now the center of my life!

THE REST OF THE STORY

I shared my story to some extent with each of the individuals mentioned in this chapter. I pointed out to them their myths and also shared how to find what they were really looking for. They then had a choice to make. Would they alter their pursuits?

I heard later that Robert decided Susan would never be the woman he desired, and he divorced her to pursue someone else he thought would be the perfect physical partner. He has since been divorced three times and is no happier than when he started his pursuit.

Charles decided not to take the job in the Middle East, but it wasn't my talk that helped as much as it was Pam's love, a love that would not part with him for any amount of monetary gain. It was God's way of helping him prayerfully realize at last that the real treasure in his life was right there at home.

Ray, the religious zealot, became a sensation in his denomination and stayed that way until his marriage fell apart. His support suddenly evaporated amid the rumor of scandal.

Then there was Lloyd. I never knew what happened to Lloyd and his wife until they attended a seminar in the southwest. I didn't expect to meet them there because they lived far away, and even when I saw them, their behavior made me sure it was just a couple who looked like them— they were so obviously in love! When I greeted them afterward, I wanted to know what had happened.

Lloyd had taken what I shared to heart and had sought out and found a vital connection with God that fulfilled and empowered him. With this accomplished, he didn't react to his wife's provocations the same way he always had. At first this infuriated her and she behaved, if possible, even worse; but he stayed on course. He not only treated her kindly, but in a God-directed way began to insist on accountability for actions and words, forcing her to communicate in a different manner. For the first time she couldn't manipulate him, couldn't even take from him this new inner peace. Slowly in her heart was born, not only a newfound respect for her husband, but also the desire to explore and understand what he had found that had so totally changed him. Nothing happened overnight, but over the course of many months their lives grew together spiritually, and things became very different in their marriage. Now they looked like a twenty-something couple, head over heels in love, instead of a couple nearing the twenty-year mark.

"How'd you end up out here?" I asked.

"Oh, that's easy. Lloyd and I are enjoying a second honeymoon at the Grand Canyon," she said with a smile and then hid her face shyly on his shoulder. They left just that way—arms around each other, ready to take on the world.

I watched them go with tears in my eyes, amazed once more at the restorative power of divine grace manifested in human flesh.

SUNSET CONVERSATION

When I worked in real estate, I met many influential and wealthy men, some of them quite famous. One of them was a man I'll call Patrick in order to protect his privacy. I met Patrick in my business, and we got to know each other fairly well. As time went on our conversations took on a deeper tone. One evening we sat gazing out at the Rocky Mountains from my front porch while the sky turned all sorts of glorious colors in the setting sun.

"Pat, I know you are worth at least a million dollars, right?" I said almost playfully.

He smiled in response and then murmured, "At least."

"And you've won all sorts of honors in your sport?"

"I won the World Championship, yes."

"You own two thriving businesses?"

"I've been very lucky," he asserted modestly, although I knew luck had little to do with the reasons for his success.

"I believe you have two homes, is that right? And one of those homes has been featured in a number of national magazines as an example not only of architecture but of style and interior design, hasn't it?"

"That is correct," he responded quietly.

"And you own the island where your vacation home sits. Furthermore, I know you have a great reputation in the business community and probably get invited to sit on some boards and committees?"

"Too many," he replied.

"You've done so much and accomplished so much more than most people do in a lifetime. What's left? Is there anything in life you haven't accomplished that you'd still like to?"

Things got very quiet on my porch that evening and stayed that way for a long time. Finally, he replied haltingly, "Jim, there are two things I have never been able to do. I've never had a marriage that works, and I've not been able to get my life right with God."

There was more to our conversation that beautiful evening, but I'll leave it there to ask you, what is the pursuit of your life? Will it bring you the satisfaction you really desire?

Only you and God can answer this, and if you are as honest as Patrick was, you have taken the first big step toward new priorities and new plans, toward the God who desires more than anything to become the love of your life. If you are willing, He will help you build a new and better life, a life you are sure to love, no matter what your circumstances or age. Unlike the myths we've been chasing, this is a truly satisfying future, and the key is empowerment—not the self-directed empowerment that is so often promoted, but a genuine empowerment by the God of all power, wisdom, and real manhood.

CHAPTER 3

THE MYTH

Questions to Consider for Personal Inventory or Group Discussion

1. When I think about myself and what I want to be known for, what comes to my mind?

2. What myths have I bought into? Which ones am I currently pursuing?
   a. The perfect sexual partner
   b. Financial success
   c. Ministry
   d. An amiable wife
   e. Hobbies
   f. Fitness
   g. The perfect location
   h. Recreation and sports
   i. Adventure
   j. A life of ease and/or partying
   k. Prestigious home and cars
   l. Any others?
3. Am I finding lasting satisfaction?
4. Do I realize that true success comes from knowing God's will for my life and living in the center of it daily?

Empowerment

Work out your own salvation with fear and trembling.
For it is God which worketh in you both to will and to do of his good pleasure.
—Philippians 2:12, 13

These two little verses contain the secret of empowerment. God is working it *in* you and me, and as He does, we are to work it *out!* It's as simple as that. This is the secret to becoming an empowered man, an empowered husband, and an empowered father. It is the key to leaving behind life's disappointing myths and finding the kernel of authentic purpose and fulfillment. It provides the fuel that fires genuine courage, true integrity, and real heart. It is so simple that even a little child can implement it; yet so profound in its application and results that the greatest men of earth have never been able to exhaust it.

God the Creator, the One who spoke and then worlds appeared, is working in me. He is working in you. He is a personal God, a heavenly Father who cares for each one of us as if there were no other. No one is exempt from His attention. Whatever your past has been, however complicated your present is, no matter how dark your future appears, He is there for you and for me. He has all the power that we need; He has all the wisdom that we need. He has the solution to every problem and the remedy for every shortcoming. There is nothing we need that He cannot supply. This is grace—the grace that saves us.[1]

---

1. See Ephesians 2:8.

So how do we tap into that? How does it work in practical terms? When God called me away from chasing my myths to pursuing Him through a wilderness experience, I didn't have the slightest idea where or how to begin. I opened God's Word to see if I could find something that would work for me. That's when Philippians 2:12, 13 came alive and I recognized the key I had been missing.

It's very simple. Each day, each moment of the day, we are to be quick to recognize the guiding voice of the Holy Spirit gently suggesting that we turn to the left or turn to the right.[2] As we respond in faith and cooperation, He supplies all we need.[3]

MISSING LINK

I used to think of grace as "unmerited favor," and this it is. But in my experience, while this definition satisfied my intellect, it remained vague in its application for my daily Christian walk. I could sing "Amazing Grace," all the while knowing in my heart that I was consistently failing to control myself—especially at home. My wife would say something I didn't like, and I'd fly off the handle and create all sorts of tension between us. Yet everyone at church thought I was an upright spiritual man. Worse still, as I looked about me in the church, all the men I knew had basically the same type of spiritual experience I had, and it frightened me to think this was all there was. I knew there had to be more to Christianity than the life we were living, full of effort and good intentions but always failing where we needed success the most. I wondered, *Is grace merely God's forgiveness for our continual failings? Or can God's grace truly empower me?*

Philippians 2:14, 15 convinced me that God's grace was intended to accomplish far more than I had yet experienced: "Do everything without complaining or arguing, so that you may be blameless and pure, children of God without fault in a crooked and depraved generation, in which you shine like stars in the universe" (NIV). I knew I couldn't measure up to this standard. No matter how hard I tried, I could not stop complaining or arguing, and I was completely incapable of over-

---

2. See Isaiah 30:21.
3. See Ephesians 2:8–10.

coming faults like irritation and anger—let alone be a shining light to the universe. If God wanted me to become like this, then there must be more to grace!

I decided to put God to the test and see if He could really deliver what His Word says. As I searched, I began to see that grace is not just some vague abstract force; rather it is God Himself saying, *"Jim, I am your Helper. You can count on Me. I will never leave you. I will never forsake you. You may have gotten into this mess by yourself, but I'll direct you out of it. Take My hand. I'll show you the way."*[4]

This truly is unmerited favor! And all of us are the objects of it. God doesn't play favorites, and the preacher has no more grace than the drunk in the ditch because God exercises His grace on behalf of all. No one can merit it; no one can earn it. Our good behavior doesn't win any brownie points with Him. He has already given Himself to us so completely that there is no more to give.

So why, then, wasn't I experiencing God's power through His grace when my Sally irritated me or my boys got on my nerves? It was simply because I didn't recognize grace when it came knocking at my door. I have since come to understand that *grace is God's continual presence in my life*—wooing me, entreating me, beckoning me, trying to save me in the present, the here and the now—in order that He may guide me, direct me, empower me, redeem me, and restore me. It is His divine influence upon my heart. But most of us resist this divine influence. Let's see how it plays out in our daily life.

INFALLIBLE COACH

I played left halfback in high school football. When the coach laid out his game plan, we followed it. As an adult I saw the parallel to my Christian walk and what a foolish player I had been. I had been playing the game of life for more than thirty years as if I were my own coach. And I wanted the Coach on the sidelines—God—to bless and prosper whatever plays I called. As far as the world judged, I was doing pretty well. But I knew in my honest heart that I was fumbling—fumbling badly. I fumbled when it came to sustaining a loving relationship

---

4. See Hebrews 13:5, 6.

with my wife; I fumbled when it came to being a real father to my boys; and I really fumbled when it came to dealing with my own character flaws.

So I made a pact with God. I'd stop running my own game plan. I'd hire Him as my exclusive Coach. I would begin immediately to let Him call the plays throughout my day. I laid my life, my marriage, and my family in His hands. I purposed to develop an ear that would be so sensitive to His still, small voice that the lightest whisper would move me into action. God knew the changes, attitudes, and approaches that needed to be made. I'd just carry them out as He'd bring them to my attention throughout my day.

Well, I soon found there was a problem with this because while God might seem very real on my knees in the quiet of the morning, temptation rarely presented itself early in the morning when I was ready for it. No, it was when the pressures of life began to build and the noise and distractions grew that my thoughts of God and what I wanted Him to do in me receded to the point of being drowned out amid the stresses and trials of life. That was when I failed over and over again, even when I knew God wanted to lead me.

I was frustrated. It was at this point my divine Coach reminded me of my football games—games with a terrible noise level and the distractions of freezing rain or snow and mud that were almost all-consuming, and yet I listened ever so carefully for the plays called so that I'd know what to do. This was a lesson I could easily apply to my personal life. I would have to develop the same sensitivity to God's grace—His still, small voice speaking to my mind.

Sometimes when a game wasn't going well, the rush and the pressure to prepare for the next play built up and built up until you could hardly pay attention to the plays being called. When that started happening we'd call a timeout. For just a brief blessed minute we'd huddle, rest, listen once more, and come out with a new plan for victory. The good news is that what works for football works in the game of life.

When we get hurried and rushed, when the devil has us pushed back and in danger, we need to call a timeout with our Coach and stop to listen, truly listen to God's voice. This is a relationship in which I trust and depend fully on another and purpose to follow all that He suggests.

Few—very few—know God in these personal terms. Almost none of us have been brought up to even realize that God's presence can be this real to us. We are very accustomed to running the game plan of our lives, including our religion. We read the Scriptures and then set out to do all that God has said in our *own* wisdom and strength. That is not Christianity. That is humanism.

Why? Because we are still in charge! We are calling our own plays and running our own games. We have become so accustomed to this mind-set that we don't realize how destructive it is to us; yet it was this very attitude that infused the heart of Lucifer and started the whole painful mess we find ourselves in today. It spread to Adam and Eve and is bound up in the heart of each and every one of us. But we don't have to stay there.

When Paul says in Romans, "The just shall live by faith,"[5] he means that we put away our self-governing and consent to live a life under divine guidance. God never expected us to do it alone. Even Jesus didn't do it alone. He emphatically stated, *"I can of mine own self do nothing."*[6]

Many sincere men and women have rejected the idea of a very personal Coach who reveals His will not just in Scripture or providence, but personally, to the individual, just as He did in Bible times when David would ask, "Shall I go?" And His Coach, the God of the universe, would tell him, *"Go,"* or *"Wait."*

God has one huge problem in trying to offer us this type of day-by-day, hour-by hour help. While we are still in charge of our lives, and as long as we remain in control, there is little He can do for us.

When I decided I wanted a deeper experience, I started searching such scriptures as "And the LORD shall guide thee continually";[7] "I will instruct thee and teach thee in the way which thou shalt go . . . I will guide thee with mine eye";[8] and "Let every man be swift to hear."[9] In such texts I saw something I had missed, and it correlated to the example I saw in the lives of the great men of the Bible. I realized they had all

---

5. Romans 1:17.
6. John 5:30, italics added.
7. Isaiah 58:11.
8. Psalm 32:8.
9. James 1:19.

come to know the voice of God as manifested not only in His Word but in their own lives. I realized that I needed to put my ear toward heaven, listen, and then implement. I needed to take the time to huddle with my Coach, hear His direction, and then go out and make the play.

TESTING IT OUT

In the lives of God's great men, long since dead, I saw the experience I longed for. Then I began experimenting. I had heard the phrase "experimental religion," but until this point I didn't know that it meant testing out what you believed God was asking you to do in the real and practical world. So I'd go to God with my struggles, study His Word to know His will, strive to discern His voice, and then try out in my experience what I thought He was telling me. At first, I still failed. I would try again and fail, but this time there was a difference in my failures. Now I was starting to learn from my mistakes, and each experiment brought me closer to God. In the past, I was doomed to failure because I didn't understand how to walk and talk with God. Now I was learning to cross over from the deeply ingrained habit of being my own coach to letting Him be the Coach. It is not something we master once and for all. It is a growing experience. Bit by bit, I began to make a little progress.

BABY STEPS

It reminds me of how I taught my boys to walk. They'd take their first baby steps forward—wobbling back and forth and side to side and eventually falling down. Do you think I would yell at them, "You dumb kid—you're never going to learn to walk. Just forget it!" No, no, a thousand times no! I'd encourage them to get back on their feet and try again. I'd be coaching on the sidelines, saying, "Come on, you can do it!" "Just one more step—you're almost there—keep coming!" "I don't care how many times you fall—I care how many times you get back up!"

That's our heavenly Father! He knows we've spent most of our lives crawling on our bellies and thinking that was the only way to get around. He understands that we have wobbly legs and poor balance when we first get on our feet and that we are prone to go back to the old familiar ways. He expects we'll fall in the process—dozens of times. But His ultimate concern is that we learn to walk. He stays with us, however long the process takes! He sees us as we will be, not as we presently are. Moreover, trying to walk and landing flat on our faces isn't wasted time but part of the process of undoing the past.

You see, unlike toddlers, we carry with us all sorts of misunderstanding and baggage from our past experience, while they are learning it right from the beginning. All of us have done things our way for so long that we have worn huge ruts in our road. When we decide at last to walk the way God wants us to, we do a lot of stumbling and falling down in the ruts of life. This should not discourage us. Trying and failing and trying again is called learning. Trying, failing, and giving up is the only real failure. Just as a toddler finally learns to walk, so we can learn to walk with God.

We all struggle here because it's foreign to us to live life in the shadow of the all-seeing One. Once we taste it, though, and successfully venture our initial steps, a new life takes over and empowers our very soul.

How it works . . .

Let me share how this works for me by taking you through a typical day. I am not your example, but perhaps my example can help you to find your own empowered walk.

The beginning of each new day represents to me the beginning of a new play in the game of life. I need time to huddle with my Coach. So I make sure I get that time. I rise about five o'clock in the morning and go for a run outside. Picture what this is like. We live in a pristine wilderness valley bordering Glacier National Park. Stalwart, craggy peaks flank us to the east, and forested mountains border the west. It is peaceful and quiet. All that greets my senses as I step out the door is directly from God's creation. As I pump my legs down the trail to the river, see glimpses of approaching dawn, or perhaps startle a browsing doe, my mind begins to tune into the One who made it all. He's there—always there! My thoughts turn to the people in my life. I bring them before Him, asking Him to guide and bless each one as He knows best. I share with Him my concerns, my need for His intervention and protection, my recognition of His constant overseeing in my life.

I return home, wide awake and alert. After showering, I go to my desk, open my Bible, and read for about half an hour. This time in God's Word is essential if I am going to recognize His voice and His principles. You see, God's voice is not the only one that calls for our attention. Our own human reasoning—what I call "self talk"—is a very strong voice, and when that is all we have, it appears right. The reasoning of others influences our thoughts and opinions. And of course, we have an enemy who is constantly working to lead us into dead-end streets. We can easily confuse these voices as God's voice and follow them, thinking we are following God. We may be sincere, but we can be sincerely wrong. God's principles as revealed in His Word provide the test for us to discern who is speaking to our hearts.

We can never exhaust the Scriptures. Just because I have read the Bible from cover to cover and know all the stories and where to find proof texts for this and that belief doesn't mean I don't need time in God's Word daily. You see, God's principles are always advancing. My understanding of how to apply a principle yesterday was sufficient for yesterday. But today, the experience needs to deepen. God's Word is always fresh, because it has the ability to reach deep into our hearts in whatever phase of experience we are in.

After about thirty minutes of time in God's Word, my mind is usually quiet. It has been emptied of "self talk" and filled with God's principles. My thinking processes are subject to His. I then enter into quiet time. I kneel down and worship God, praising Him for who He is and thanking Him for His hand in my life and in the lives of others. I talk to Him as to a friend, sharing my joys, concerns, heartaches, and plans. I confess my shortcomings and ask for His cleansing and empowering grace. I commit to be sensitive to my conscience, according to the principles of His Word throughout my day. Most important, I *listen*.

Most people approach God as some kind of divine errand boy and give Him a list of what they want Him to do for them. While there is certainly room in prayer for sharing our needs with God, it is far more vital for us to consciously turn our life over to God. Rather than telling Him what to do, we need to cultivate a willingness on our part to enter into *listening for Him* throughout our day. We don't control God. We can't say, "Here I am now—I've got ten minutes. Whisper to me my instructions for the day." That's controlling God.

I give God opportunity to impress my mind while I am on my knees. If my mind is not quiet, I will use a text of Scripture to focus my mind on God's will for me. If I am wrestling with something, I often will go outside for a walk and talk aloud to God. This communion is essential to make me sensitive to His guidance throughout my day and to motivate me to act as He prompts.

BALANCING THE ROADRUNNER

Over the years, I have found that quieting the background noise of my life has helped me be more attentive to my Coach. I am, by nature, training, and preference, a roadrunner. My Trainer has worked with me here to slow my pace and find balance because when I run too fast, I don't hear Him calling to my heart so easily. The automatic responses to life tend to take over. Therefore, I have eliminated the TV, the radio, newspapers, and magazines. Many people have difficulty in a quiet environment, but I have come to relish quietness because I can more readily discern the voice of my Coach directing me to the winning play. As I cooperate in this way, a new sense of God's presence in my life begins to shine in. As I begin to walk in the light of it, my mannerisms change. My disposition to others becomes refined. My thoughtfulness to put others' needs before my own takes on a new dimension. I step out and find that God's ways are better than my ways. This is what it means to have a living faith—a connected faith to a present Savior.

OFF MY KNEES, ON MY LEGS

Now it's time to go out into my day. As I walk out of my little study I glance into the bedroom that Sally and I share and see that the bed is unmade. I have learned that when you allow God to be in charge of your life, He asks you to do things your natural inclinations do not want to do. I start walking down the stairs, but the uneasiness in my heart gently suggests I go back up and make the bed.

But, Lord . . . that's Sally's job!

"Who's in control, Jim?" The decision is always mine.

Well, Lord, I suppose it would be a nice gesture to my Sally.

"Yes, Jim, she'd really appreciate it."

OK, Lord. Not my will, but Yours be done. Let's make the bed.[10]

It's just this simple. A sensitivity to God's will versus my will.

Five minutes later, I'm ready for our family worship. We sing a song, kneel for prayer, read several paragraphs that encourage us in the Christian way and discuss in detail their meaning to us. We close with prayer, and Sally begins the meal preparation.

I start heading for my desk to begin my duties for the day. But as I glance over my shoulder I see my Sally trying not only to prepare the meal, but also to fold the laundry, put another load in, and put the clothes away. That still, small voice of my Coach is saying, *"She sure could use some help and encouragement."*

But, Lord . . . I really want to get to my day—not hers!

We are all very self-centered in one way or another. For me it seems that getting things done is more important than people. I have an imbalance. We're all out of balance to the left or to the right. But will I consent to swing to the middle? I contemplate this for a few moments and surrender my choice to my Coach. Sally is touched as she sees me cleaning up the kitchen and putting the clothes away. I love the big smile coming out of her heart and shining through her countenance. Love at night begins—always begins—by love during and throughout the day. Not that this is our motivation or focus, but it's a reality of why so many men wrestle with a cool partner in the evening. Come on, guys. Think of it. If the roles were reversed, tell me how warm you'd be to a husband who shuns you throughout your day and chases you at night?

We have a lovely meal together, not with TV, newspaper, radio, or the like absorbing our attention, but communication regarding our lives, our children, our future. It's live, open, invigorating. We do the dishes together, and my Sally's cup is full. She's cheery and in love. My actions in obedience to my Coach encourage her. How few wives ever receive even this much consideration in their day? No wonder the mar-

---

10. See Luke 22:42.

riage is stale and lackluster. Moreover, what kind of ministry would I have if I wrote and spoke about the Christian life but treated Sally like a convenience at home?

All I did was listen to my Coach on what play to run next. Hey, guys, it's not complicated. But it does require a death to my will and my way in the moment. It's called living in the shadow of our Savior. Now your situation may vary and your circumstances may be different, but the principle is the same. "Nevertheless not as I will, but as thou wilt."[11]Here I am, Lord; use me as a tool of Your righteousness. May I not merely live for myself, but for the benefit of my loved ones every day for the rest of my life.

This goes beyond religion and deals with the heart of Christianity, which is Calvary. Calvary represents laying down my life for the benefit of others. I don't want you to think that this is miserable. On the contrary, I'm probably the happiest husband and father in this world, the most fulfilled man. It is hard to make the crossover from a self-run life to a divinely coached life. But the dividends of a marriage that's revitalized and refreshed and a family that's tight and together are great.

ROADRUNNER VS. TURTLE

At last, I am able to start work at my desk. I often face monumental tasks, just like you do in your professions. The ministry God has called us into has grown, and it involves many people participating in their specific tasks. As I said, I'm a roadrunner who likes to get things done. The problem is that some of those I work with are turtles, and they need time to be creative. God created both turtles and roadrunners. However, the roadrunners can pressure turtles to the point that they just want to hide in their shells, and the turtles can get so caught up in being creative that they forget the goal is to cross the finish line.

This particular day I was following up on some DVDs, but it could just as easily have been a detail about a CD or something with the publishing work. Invariably someone somewhere drops the ball, and it is my misfortune to be the one to pick up the fumbles and carry them forward. Recently I had to call a turtle who seems to have two speeds—

11. Matthew 26:39.

late or later, and only two gears—delayed or derailed entirely. This project has already had its deadline set back once, and now all I'm getting are excuses. I feel the danger of my resorting to the flesh, rather than dealing with this man in the Spirit. It would be all too easy for me as the roadrunner to run over this turtle, and I realize it. I don't know where you find yourself in this scenario—if you're the turtle that needs to shed its shell or the roadrunner that needs to slow down. In either case, they both need to come to the center in Jesus. They both need an empowering shift of natures, a divine Coach overseeing them.

I made my call, and I could sense the tension mounting. This is where most of us lose our dependence and take things into our own hands. We seem to let Jesus' presence fade away as we increasingly rely upon our own thoughts, emotions, abilities, and problem-solving techniques or lack thereof.

TOUCHDOWN!

I paused on the phone, my silence speaking volumes. What am I doing? I am consulting my Coach for a fresh approach that will see us both to the finish line as part of the same team.

This is what I call the great exchange. It's when I take my problems to God and trade them for His peace and His solution. When I first started, it could take me fifteen or twenty minutes to gain self-control in Christ, but now I can obtain what I seek in just a few moments. I'm like a runner who starts running a ten-minute mile, then with training drops his time to eight minutes and then six minutes, and finally moves toward a four-minute mile. So, too, in the Christian life, those things that took a long time at the beginning take less and less time as we gain proficiency.

Suddenly, I sense a new idea and say to my turtle friend, "What would you do if you were me? I am frustrated and need your help."

I can feel a change in attitude on the other end of the phone as his attitude softens and he begins to seek a solution with me. He replies, "I hear your dilemma, Jim. Let me think it over, and I'll call you back."

Now my work is not finished. God would bring my lesson closer still and have me pray for this man as he mulls over our situation. I find myself praying, "Lord, by Your grace—Your presence, Your wisdom,

Your strength—touch this man in a way that moves his soul. Help me to remain rested in You regardless of the outcome. Help me to understand that character is what You are interested in more than the finish line and that this work is Yours and not mine to carry out."

I can't pray for another man like this without my heart being drawn out toward his, and in place of frustration I am cultivating a deep and sincere interest in the individual as a precious human being. This is the secret that keeps Jesus from fading away in the cares of my day and keeps me from allowing my emotions, my thoughts, and my wisdom to take over. This great exchange—this trading of my thoughts, feelings, and emotions for my Coach's wisdom and game plan—scores a touchdown!

The great exchange awaits us at all times and places, but it's up to us to call a timeout if the day, the circumstances, or the feelings are taking us over. For me, it's a pause in the midst of the battle just to remind myself of who's in charge. When we are motivated enough to filter all through our divine Coach, the great exchange occurs. This is the empowerment that's ours, but it's only ours as we plug into the power source—again and again and again.

My turtle eventually calls back, assuring me my material will be on its way in twenty-four hours, and I hope that he will follow through. Whether he does or not, I can remain rested rather than frustrated.

SWING TIME

Now it's noon, and my day has drained me. But it has also energized me. I invite my wife for some swing time on our outdoor swing. While we sip on a cool glass of mountain fresh spring water, I'm tempted to carry the baggage of my skepticism over my turtle into our conversation. My Coach suggests, *"Jim—refresh your wife. Don't add this baggage to her day. Ask her how the new chapter in her book is going. Keep the conversation proactive, not reactive."*

This is a new play. Again, my Coach is calling for a choice. It seems my life is made up of a bundle of choices. God says, "Choose you this day *whom* ye will serve."[12] That's the true Christian life. It

---

12. Joshua 24:15; italics added.

goes beyond a mere belief and deals with a life of faith, surrender, and dependence upon the One—the only One who loves us with an eternal love.

HE'S INVOLVED

In the afternoon, one of my tasks is to put up several bluebird nesting boxes down in the new meadow that was created by the forest fire on the corner of our property. I gather together the tools and materials I think I'll need, including a small pair of wire snips.

A thought impresses my mind, *"Why don't you take along your large wire snips, too?"*

That's a stupid idea, I think. *I only need the small ones. The staples on these bird houses are small.* I promptly dismiss the idea and march off to complete my task.

A quarter mile away from my garage, I hang those bird houses. To complete the job, I need to pull out several small staples, and to do so, I pick up my small wire snips. I begin to apply them to the task, but find they won't work because one of the tips has broken off. I have to walk all the way back to my garage to retrieve my large pair. On the way, I marvel at my Coach's care for me. He gets involved with even the small details of my life and wants to save me from my shortsightedness—if only I would listen. I renew my willingness to be directed by Him.

TIMEOUT

The rest of the afternoon, I get bombarded by phone calls, an unexpected guest, and a big disappointment. Our generator, which is our only source of electricity, is sputtering. I get almost nothing done that afternoon that I wanted done. All that I did do is under the *tyranny of the urgent.* I like getting my things done!

At six-thirty in the evening my wife looks at me with those searching eyes that say, "You don't need more tasks to do. Let's go for a long walk down to the river."

I wrestle inside. I'd rather fix the generator. The roadrunner inside me is chafing at the bit and wanting free rein. I'm tempted to say, "Go without me. I've got too much on my plate."

But I sense a still, small Voice saying, *"Come ye yourself apart and rest a while."*[13] Again, the struggle is for who will be in charge. I know what I should do, but it's not a matter of knowledge. It is a matter of application. Will I apply myself to the work that lies nearest or succumb to the tyranny of the urgent? My vote is cast.

"Let's go! The generator can wait until tomorrow."

My roadrunner is subdued. God wins, my marriage wins, and I win, too!

As I go to bed that night, I realize there's been a hand in my life that, if given full sway, will work in me a new character, a revitalized marriage, and a restored family. How can I say no? How audacious of me to think I could ever have managed my life on my own. How longsuffering has been my Lord to wait for me to take notice of His supreme interest in my welfare!

What was the difference between Peter and Judas? Both were disciples of Christ and enjoyed His inner circle of friendship. Both had serious character flaws. Both were accustomed to being their own coach. Both were given the opportunity to relinquish management of their own lives and to give Christ control. Peter crossed over. Judas did not. Whose path are you following?

"LORD, WHAT WILT THOU HAVE ME TO DO?"

If you realize that you have been running your own game, why not cross over right now? Why not try it for just thirty days? What do you have to lose? For just thirty days, simply focus on the question Saul asked when he finally stopped running his own game plan and began listening to his divine Coach: "Lord, what wilt thou have me to do?"[14] That's the question to be asked when you rise up, when you carry on your day, and when you lie down. Just let God have you—as much as you can—for thirty days. Play out only His game plan as you understand it. Make your wife and your children a priority over yourself. Live to honor His name in every conversation and every activity throughout your day.

---

13. See Mark 6:31.
14. Acts 9:6.

What you'll find is amazing. I have challenged scores of men to try this life-changing program, and many of them come back to me and say, "God is real . . . He is there . . . He does speak to me! My wife, my children, and my friends all say they see a difference in my life. I'm recognizing where I've wounded my loved ones, and I'm finding the power to heal them instead. I thought I'd feel so restricted. Instead, I feel so free!"

Come on! Get on board! Thirty days isn't long! Simply let go and let God be your Coach!

CHAPTER 4
EMPOWERMENT

Questions to Consider for Personal Inventory or Group Discussion

1. What did the Holy Spirit say to me as I read this chapter? Will I respond?
2. Will my understanding of grace make a difference in my daily experience?
3. If someone were to ask my wife who was running my game plan, what would she say? Am I man-managed or God-governed?
4. What dulls my consciousness of God?
5. What busyness in my life needs to be quieted down?
6. As I enter my day and interact with my loved ones, would they say that they see me yielding to my divine Coach?
7. Do they experience the practical results of me listening to my divine Coach?
8. When I think about my work, what is most important to me— getting the job done, or finding my center in Jesus?
9. When the Holy Spirit whispers in my ear, do I respond consistently?
10. What is my response to the thirty-day challenge?

Wounding Their Spirits

A brother offended is harder to be won than a strong city:
and their contentions are like the bars of a castle.
—Proverbs 18:19

It was one of *those* days at work. Everything seemed to be going wrong. I had clients with problems, staff issues, a phone that rang constantly, and a pile of paperwork on my desk that seemed endless. By afternoon my head was pounding, I had a kink in my neck, and all I wanted to do was to go home, collapse in my recliner, and just vegetate.

I didn't know what was taking place in my home as I plodded mechanically through my stress-filled day at the office, but as my wife, Sally, went about her work, she chatted with our four-year-old, Matthew.

"Matthew, did you know that Father will be having a birthday in just four days? Wouldn't it be fun to plan something special for him?"

Matthew's eyes sparkled, and the gears in his fertile little mind began to turn. He loved his daddy and was old enough to know that birthdays were special, fun occasions. He began to think of all the things he could do for Daddy's birthday. First, he drew some pictures for me and put them in a shoebox. There was still a lot of room in that box, so he went outside and gathered some treasures from nature that he was sure I would like. He enthusiastically wrapped that precious little box as only a four-year-old can and topped it with a bow. Then he waited anxiously for me to come home. Four days is an eternity to a four-year-old, and there was no way he was going to wait that long to give me my present. It was all he could bear just to wait until the end of the day! He just knew Father would be as excited about the gift as he was.

When he heard my car drive in, he ran to meet me at the door full of anticipated pleasure. I strode in with one thing on my mind—vegetating in my recliner! I barely noticed the excited little boy as I brushed him aside and headed for the living room. He followed me, and when I was finally settled, he stood before me, unable to contain his surprise any longer.

"Father, Father!" he half shouted. "I have a birthday present for you!"

I peered at him through tired eyes and a throbbing headache, and all the tension of the day broke loose.

"Matthew, just leave me alone!" I commanded harshly. "Besides, it's *not* my birthday."

Even with my neck kinking, I could see his little face fall as the rejection sank in. His pleasure, excitement, and anticipation drained right out through his toes. Heartbroken, he retreated to hide his tears in his mother's arms. His spirit closed to me.

POKING THE POOR TURTLE

We've all done it, haven't we? We've all found ourselves speaking harshly to the ones we love. "You stupid fool; look at what you just did." "Can't you do anything right?" "If I've told you once, I've told you a thousand times." "Can't you open your eyes?" "What is wrong with you?" I remember once coming upon a group of boys who were teasing a turtle. They all were poking that poor turtle with sticks and, of course, he had pulled into his shell and wouldn't come out for anything. That's what happens to our children and wives when we poke them with harsh, thoughtless words. Some may retreat into silence while others react with anger, but all close their spirits against us—and that's just what Matthew did.

You know, I was a "Christian," the head elder in the church, when I treated Matthew so harshly. I had a good grasp of sound biblical doctrine, lived a conservative lifestyle, and was active in outreach and evangelism. Yet this was not sufficient to keep me from building a wall between me and one of the people I treasure most. Since that day, I have found that there are literally dozens of ways in which we can close off the spirits or hearts of our loved ones, and I think I've done my share of them, but in this chapter, I'll touch on just a few.

"YOU STUPID FOOL!"

A friend of mine was building a house, and his wife volunteered to help him. She had virtually no experience but was eager and willing. He asked her to support the end of a 4 × 8 sheet of plywood as he ran it through the table saw. As the sheet came through the saw, she attempted to support both sides of the cut, but in her inexperience she allowed the ends to sag, making the final cut awkward.

"What's wrong with you?" he yelled. "Don't you know how to hold a sheet of plywood?"

"I thought I was holding it. You didn't tell me there was anything special to know about it."

"Well, it should be obvious for anyone with eyes!" he sneered sarcastically as he grabbed the piece of lumber and stomped away.

This type of attitude closes the heart and kills honest communication. It sends a message of superiority, saying, "I'm smart. You're stupid. Can't you get your act together?" Volatile emotional outbursts destroy the trust and confidence so necessary to good communication and yes, even affection.

Nagging our loved ones, hoping it will motivate them to come into line, does the same thing. "You never clean your room." "You never do your chores right." "You are never on time." "You always burn the toast." "You never remember to turn the heat down when you leave." "You never want to go out like we used to." "You're never interested anymore." "You always leave a mess." Any time the words *never* or *always* enter our vocabulary, it spells hurt!

BUILDING WALLS—BRICK UPON BRICK

Another way we hurt the ones we love is often completely nonverbal. It happens when we treat their ideas and opinions as if they really don't matter; we roll our eyes when they are talking, or just wear an impatient or disgusted look. This communicates loudly that we can't wait for them to get their stupid idea out of the way. Sometimes we even respond incredulously, "Where did you ever get that from?"

It wounds them afresh, doesn't it? They feel rejection, and another brick is added to the wall that is slowly but surely separating us.

Being too busy to care about them or to listen to them is perhaps the easiest way we shut out those we care about. The enemy of our souls has diligently worked to bring unnumbered demands upon our time and attention, leaving us physically worn and mentally exhausted. We get so focused upon the *urgent* that we don't even recognize the subtle hints for attention from our loved ones. I know I have. "Not now . . . later." "Later . . . when I am not so pressured." "Later . . . when things calm down." But later never comes, and they wait and they wait until they discover the world has time for them; until our children discover a young man or woman who has time for them; or even until our wife discovers another man who has the time for her when we were too busy, too stressed, too tired, too ambitious, too self-important, or perhaps just too blind to give them the time they longed for so desperately.

Doing the right things in the wrong way is often the bane of parenting. Discipline—every child needs it. Most parents try to provide it, but many of us fail miserably to benefit either the child or the family because we discipline when we are angry. We demand rather than teach, intimidate rather than instruct, and then to top it off, we insult them when they fail, even in front of their friends, because they may not understand what we think they ought to or we don't give them credit for knowing and understanding as much as they do. "Because I said so" is not a very compelling reason! In spite of our own great self-image, our children see us as we are—warts and all. And usually they love us anyway, unless we've so wounded their hearts that they no longer can. Somehow, we must break the chain, stop the cycle, and do things differently. Through the empowering grace of God, we can.

REFLEXIVE RECOIL

Sally and I once walked up to a house where a cute little dog was playing in the yard. I love animals, but when I reached down to pet it, the poor little thing cowered and shrank back! "Let me try," Sally offered, and bent over to pet the dog. It responded warmly, delightedly wagging its tail.

"Well, look at that!" I exclaimed. "Let me try now." Again the little dog whimpered and pulled away.

Sally looked at me sadly and remarked, "The man in this home mistreats this dog."

I've met a lot of children who are like this little dog, cowering while they anticipate the next insult or harsh word. Others are like that turtle, withdrawn into a hard, protective shell that nobody gets past. Some go through the motions, but their spirits are closed. My heart goes out to these young people, and I try to draw them out whenever I can. In the process, I have found that the common thread of a wounded spirit runs through their individual stories.

DRIVING THEM AWAY

Cassy was a lovely, well-mannered fifteen-year-old I met at a weekend seminar. She longed to share her hopes, dreams, goals, and feelings with her parents, but they were simply noncommunicative and unavailable. I met her parents—nice, sincere people just as their daughter described them. Her father was a minister, and her mother a schoolteacher. They had a fantastic reputation in their community for their work and abilities. They were frustrated with their daughter, who was involved with a young man whose character was, in her parents' judgment, questionable. They just couldn't understand why she'd share her affections with a "loser" like that.

I could see why very quickly. Her "loser" boyfriend was there for her; he listened to her, laughed with her, spent time with her. He saw value in her. She'd never experienced this before. It wasn't surprising that Cassy mistakenly thought she was in love. Her feet hardly touched the ground because, for the first time in her life, her basic emotional needs were being fulfilled. Sadly, many young women are swept off their feet this way. What about yours? Are you leaving an emotional vacuum in your daughter's heart or your son's heart or your wife's heart? Do you really want to leave them vulnerable to those who would take advantage of them?

Luke was as nice a teenager as you'd ever come across when I first met him, and yet it seemed his parents were always riding him about one thing or another. Born to his father's first marriage, he found himself now in a blended family with his father, his stepmother, and their son. Being "his" in a family of "ours" was hard enough, but to even a casual observer, the stepmother gave preference to her own flesh and blood, was too quick to blame the older boy, and too slow to correct her own child's flaws. His father sided with the stepmother, and Luke found no safe place to go except into his turtle shell. He could never please, never gain approval, never be accepted. The hurt grew. What began as simple protective withdrawal grew into rebellious and antisocial behavior. His parents saw this as the final proof of his guilt as the troublemaker. When he was eighteen, he left home, his relationship with his parents virtually destroyed, not because Luke set out to be bad but because they continually wounded his spirit. What about the Lukes in your life? Are they finding a safe place in you?

Brian had a winning personality and a ready smile, so it was only as we got to know this nineteen-year-old better did we come to realize that he had major issues with his parents. Raised and home-schooled by a religious but relatively poor West Virginia farm family, his experience in the world was admittedly scant. He had, however, the desire any young man has to make something out of himself—to be somebody— but his upbringing had not treated him kindly. Due to poor organization, his home-school education was lacking, probably amounting to something less than eight full grades, even though he was now a full-grown man. He was working to get his GED so he could consider college, but he hadn't many study skills and found himself more interested in the pretty girls than in his books. He felt left behind by his peers and resentful of his parents, who let him enter adulthood with so many strikes against him. His parents' failure to reckon with the missing elements in their home training communicated a subtle yet strong message that he was not worth investing in—a message he will likely struggle with for a lifetime.

What about you? Did you receive similar messages while you were growing up? Are you passing them on?

One man told me about his children and confessed in a moment of insight, "Our children do not leave home; we drive them away." What is the Holy Spirit saying to you right now? In what ways do you build walls with your loved ones?

CHECKLIST

The following is a summary of ten prominent ways that we most often use to wound those we love. As you scan the list, I encourage you to write down what God impresses upon you. If you are willing to dig even deeper and have the courage to be vulnerable, share this list with your wife and children and ask for their feedback.

- Is your son, daughter, or wife offended on a regular basis?
- Is there contention in your family?
- Do you lecture them?
- Do you use harsh words?
- Do you respond to them as though their opinions don't really matter?
- Are you too *busy* to listen to them or answer them?
- Do you discipline in anger?
- Do you say no without giving a reason?
- Do you insult them in front of others?
- Do you yell at them when they already know they are wrong?

If you recognize this eroding process happening in your relationships, if you sense the hearts of your children or your spouse are closing to you, there is hope! It is based on five solid biblical principles that are absolutely guaranteed to work—when you apply them.

1. " 'LORD, WHAT DO YOU WANT ME TO DO?' " (ACTS 9:6, NKJV).

This is simply the principle of empowerment that we discussed in detail in the last chapter. It means putting God in charge of me—fully, completely, entirely. He is in charge of my thoughts, my emotions, everything that comes out of my mouth, and everything I express non-verbally. I remain open to His input all through the day, and as He makes me aware of closing the spirit of another, I can enter into the

Great Exchange. I give Him the way that doesn't work, and He points out a fresh approach.

Of course, this is awkward at first, but making repeated decisions to yield to God and a cultivated awareness of His voice speaking to us develops a sensitive conscience. It was this attitude that Joshua displayed when he said, "What saith my lord unto his servant?"[1]

Remember my friend who spoke harsh words to his wife over her ignorance in helping him at the table saw? As you can imagine, his wife regretted that she had ever offered to help him in the first place. She withdrew to a safe distance, and he wondered why. The next morning as he asked God to search his heart, the Holy Spirit pointed out his attitude of harsh superiority and impressed on him the need to apologize. He struggled with his pride but finally swallowed it and approached his wife.

"I was wrong, honey. I had no right to speak to you that way—even if I had told you the right way to hold it. Will you forgive me?"

Tears welled up in her eyes, and the wall came down. Warmth replaced the coolness, and a smile brightened the sad countenance. That wasn't hard, was it? Oh, it was hard on that man's flesh, but it wasn't complicated. God has solutions that work, if only we will listen and obey.

2. "A soft answer turns away wrath" (Proverbs 15:1, NKJV).

Gentleness has a way of melting away hurt, anger, and rebellion. You remember my little boy Matthew and his present that I rejected and how heartbroken he was? Well, as I sat in my chair and tried to relax, I felt absolutely terrible, as only one who has been totally and foolishly wrong can feel. I could hear the Lord calling to my heart to make things right, so I went to him, apologized for my behavior, and asked him gently and kindly to show me my present.

Sally encouraged him back toward me, and soon he was sitting on my lap and helping me open the present. When I showed true interest in him, when I was tender and loving, when I showed I cared about his

---

1. Joshua 5:14.

gift and about him, he relaxed and the wall that had gone up between us when I uttered my harsh words came back down.

Perhaps you know someone who needs to hear tender words from you. If so, don't put it off. When we are surrendered to Christ, His tenderness can flow through us, and the results can be profound.

One more caution, especially for your teenagers who have felt hurt a lot longer than my little Matthew did at four and may not respond as quickly as he did. They may also have some harsh and hurtful words of their own to spew back. Have patience and keep coming back with a soft answer. Don't pressure them to open up right away. They need to see that you are truly safe and trustworthy before they poke their head out of their shell.

3. " 'COME NOW, AND LET US REASON TOGETHER' " (ISAIAH 1:18, NKJV).

Spouses, friends, even children often dream long and desire more than anything else that someday, someone will understand them—what they are feeling, what they think, and how they are hurting. Often they don't even care if you disagree, as long as they know someone understands and cares. It has been my experience and the experience of countless men I have counseled that if we give our loved ones time, encouragement, and openness, they can and usually do tell us how they feel. A friend of mine tells me that if you really want to know how his wife feels, you have to go for at least a three-mile walk with her. It takes her three miles of communication to reach the stage where she can really share what's on her heart.

When there is this type of trust and intimate communication, then you can begin to reason together and to work on solutions together. Sometimes it takes this kind of commitment if we are to get to the hearts of our wives, children, or friends. You might have to initiate several *l-o-n-g* walks with them, might have to initiate many conversations, might have to shut up and let them talk, or gently prod them to share.

In our family, one of the best ways we've found to prevent misunderstandings and harsh words is to have a prearranged way to deal with problems and grievances that each may feel from time to time.

We call them family councils. Anyone, no matter how young, could request a family council to address any concern they had, and the whole family would consider their problem or complaint. Everyone gets a chance to speak and express themselves without any fear of retribution, as long as it's done respectfully. Once the problem has been stated, no one is allowed to speak unless they offer a solution. This eliminates the endless debates and self-justifying that makes the proverbial "mountain out of a molehill" and brings us no nearer the solution.

I remembered the day Matthew had requested a family council. I could tell he was upset, but I could think of nothing I had done to ruffle his feathers, so I concluded it had to be his mother or brother who was in "trouble," so to speak. Therefore, when the time came for us to get together, I was astonished when he looked straight at me and said, "It's you, Father. You used my new chain saw without asking me."

I must confess that I was strongly tempted to justify myself—after all, I am the man of the house and I can do what I want, right? But as I sat there and prayerfully considered what he was saying, I remembered I had always insisted that my boys ask to use my tools. Requiring them to be accountable for their use of my tools was one way I instilled in them a sense of responsibility and respect for personal property. Now Matthew had purchased his first major tool. That morning I had been working outside and had just a couple of small limbs to cut up. When I went to get my saw, his was sitting beside mine. It was so small and cute; I thought it would be easier than getting out my bigger one, and besides, who doesn't want to try a shiny new tool? So, without another thought, I borrowed it for those few cuts. Matthew heard his saw running and watched me using it. He was offended that I hadn't asked him.

"Well, Matthew, I don't have a biblical text for this, but when I was growing up we were always taught that what's good for the goose is good for the gander. I'm sorry I took your saw without asking. Please forgive me. In the future I will ask you."

That was all it took. His sense of injustice melted away, and harmony was restored. It was just a little thing, but it is almost always little things neglected that fracture relationships and yield a harvest of bitterness and misery.

That brings us to our next principle:

4. "If we confess our sins, He is faithful and just to forgive us our sins" (1 John 1:9, NKJV).

When I was writing this chapter I went to my boys because I needed an illustration of a time when I had hurt their feelings and manifested an irritated or overbearing spirit. In general terms I knew I had lost my self-control many times, and many times had to go back and make things right with them. I remembered it being one of the hardest things I ever had to do, and believe me, I seemed to have to do it a lot!

So I asked the boys, figuring they'd remember at least some incidents. Andrew was thoughtful and then said, "I know there were times, but I can't think of any specifics."

Matthew didn't even pause. "I just forgive and forget," he exclaimed cheerfully, as if I were half crazy to think he harbored bad feelings or even memories about me.

In a way, they were perhaps right. They understood forgiveness better than I had given them credit for. I was no nearer an illustration, but, praise God, I found out in the process that there were no hidden hurts between my sons and me. How much better to endure the momentary humiliation of admitting we're wrong and confessing our faults than to reap a lifelong harvest of alienation.

5. "He that handleth a matter wisely shall find good" (Proverbs 16:20).

We find "good" when we set out to stop hurting each other—when we take the time to filter our responses to our loved ones through our heavenly Father. Real wisdom seldom arises from our "knee-jerk" responses to life. If we will only pause before reacting, our Coach can lead us to handle matters wisely. Opening up communication is hard—especially if there have been few words except some harsh or hurtful words for a long time. However, it can be done. I don't think it is ever too late to go to the ones we love and ask if we've done or are doing anything that offends them. And if we ask questions like this, we must be sure to give them plenty of time to respond and really listen to what they are saying—without correcting the details. Their perspective has validity, even if it's different from ours.

I know one man who felt his habit of speaking harshly was so ingrained that at first he didn't trust himself to speak, and he started writing loving notes to his family. Whatever it takes, don't let these wounds fester another day. You can pick up these principles and begin to apply them today—like a man named Charlie did.

DON'T WAIT ANOTHER DAY!

Charlie was not a church-goer, and he had never been to one of my seminars. He was the national sales manager for a large company and was in our area supervising the local salesman, Reggie, who happened to be a good friend of ours. As they were checking out a display in one of the stores, Reggie was enthusiastically telling Charlie about us—our move to the mountains, our walk with God, and our family. Just then we walked around the corner, and Reggie was delighted to introduce us.

Charlie seemed anything but interested, but we invited him to come up for breakfast the next morning. He was noncommittal, so we told him we would set a place for him and if he showed up, fine. If not, no problem. Well, he showed up! He really plied us with questions and eye-balled our boys. After a lively visit, he arose to leave. I felt impressed to offer him two of my presentations on CD and gave them to him, telling him that if he was only going to toss them aside, I wouldn't have him bother. If he would listen to them, he could take them as a gift. He accepted them.

Nearly two months went by before I received the following letter from Charlie.

Dear Jim,

Thanks so much for allowing me to visit you in October. I do want you to know that it was a wonderful experience for me, one I will never forget. As we dwell in the day-to-day secular world, many of us fail to see what really matters.

You gave me two CDs of your messages. I listened to the one on simplification first and had to laugh here and there, because we all get caught up so easily in the material things from time to time. I certainly know what you meant and while we've never been deeply materialistic, we still pursue "things" when we should be pursuing the relationship with each other and God that has been offered us. This message was a gentle reminder to get back on track.

I must be honest about the second message, *Wounding Their Spirits*. While I could laugh a little at the first CD I wasn't laughing at this one. It hurt. A lot! But it only did because you were talking to me. I wish I had heard that sermon fifteen years ago; it would have saved me the trouble of learning these things the hard way.

The first thing I did when I got home that week was to sit down with my wife and children and apologize to them for wounding their spirits for so many years and committing to them that I was going to change. In many ways I have been a good father to them and I think they would agree, but in the most important aspects I have not been. I shared with them your sermon and my regret at not having heard it many years before. However we all know the Lord gives us a chance to change if our hearts are committed to that change; and I am!

In the past six weeks we have had better walks and talks as a family than we have had in fifteen years. I sincerely appreciate the message you gave me that day, and I and my family will never forget it!
Sincerely,
Charlie

Charlie is a courageous man! You can be too. If God is impressing you that you are wounding your loved ones, don't be discouraged and don't be complacent. That's what God's empowering grace is all about. Simply acknowledge where you fall short—first of all to Him and then to those who have been hurt. Put God in charge of you, and what He works *in* your mind, work *out* in your relationships. If you find yourself falling back into the old ways, don't give up. Remember, God isn't so concerned with how many times you fall as He is with how many times you get back up. The dividends you will reap as the walls come down will more than repay you. May God bless you with the courage to face yourself, the integrity to make things right where needed, the heart to feel for your loved ones, and the purpose to be all He made you to be!

CHAPTER 5

WOUNDING THEIR SPIRITS

Questions to Consider for Personal Inventory or Group Discussion

1. Is this a problem in my family?
2. Do I wound my wife on a consistent basis?
3. Which of the areas listed in the chapter checklist apply in my home?
4. Do I spend time with them daily to meet their personal needs?
5. Have I attempted to clear up the old wounds of the past?
6. Do I know how to reopen my relationships?
    a. "Lord, what do You want me to do?"
    b. "A soft answer turns away wrath."
    c. "Come now, and let us reason together."
    d. "If we confess our sins, He is faithful and just to forgive us our sins."
    e. He that handleth a matter wisely shall find good."
7. Will I vow to keep a clear slate with all my loved ones?
8. What action is God asking me to take now?

Family First

He must manage his own family well and see that his children obey him with
proper respect. (If anyone does not know how to manage his own family,
how can he take care of God's church?)
—1 Timothy 3:4, 5, NIV

A farmer was plowing his field near a canal. The day was hot, and the
bank of the stream made an inviting place for his son to play. The little
one happily tossed rocks and sticks into the swift flowing current while
his father plowed round after slow round, leaving a small cloud of dust
in his wake. Every now and then the farmer would check his son's location, concerned about the spring run-off in the canal, but when he saw
that all was well, he relaxed and let his mind dwell on getting the field
ready to plant.

Suddenly all was *not* well.

"Help! Dad, help!"

Glancing in the direction of the desperate cry, the father saw that his
son had disappeared. Quickly he stood up on the moving tractor and
could just pick out his son's hand grasping the slender, low-hanging
branch of a willow. The cold, muddy current was sucking the boy's legs
downstream and slowly but surely loosening his grip on the twig. This
was the supreme moment of danger that all fathers dread. Action is required. The farmer shouted encouragement to his child.

"Hang on, son! Hang on . . . until I plow another round!"

Unbelievable, you say. I wish it were. But friends, that was me! And most likely, it is you. How can I say that? I can say that because I see it happening all over!

Fathers are too wrapped up in the cares of life and their own selfish interests—their Internet surfing, their pet issues, their hobbies, their reading, their friends, their sports, their whatever—while their loved ones struggle against the swift flowing current of life that is about to overpower and drown them.

Businessmen are too busy to tend to the real needs of their families. These men don't run their businesses—their businesses run them. Their businesses possess them. They live for their businesses.

Ministers, preachers, evangelists, ministry leaders, and church administrators are tending to the outward needs of their congregations, their churches, the whole world, in fact, while the inward needs of their own families are neglected, ignored, and bypassed for a seemingly more promising or important crop.

Our families are floundering while we are reluctant to get off our tractors, and yet the family is the very foundation of society. If the family fails, society falls apart. Families are unique in the structure of the civilization in that no county, state, or federal program can fix them, not even if billions of dollars were invested annually.

Why? Because it is not dollars that are needed. It is *dads* that are needed! Dads who are real fathers in every sense of the word; dads who will say to their families, "Hang on! I'll be right there! Hang on! I'm coming now! Hang on, I'll be with you and we'll get out of the ditch together, one step at a time. Take my hand and I'll show you the way!" Our children need to hear this when peers pressure them to compromise. Our wives need to hear this when they are tired or troubled.

MESSED UP!

Instead, the men of today are messed up. They are messed up because they are no longer the patriarchs of their homes, no longer the priests of their families, sometimes not even the protectors or providers. In fact, in far too many homes, Dad is simply absent! A man who fails in these basic roles is messed up regardless of his achievements in the political, professional, or sports arena. Our families are in trouble today because no one is fixing Dad!

When Dad is messed up, you have a messed-up family. Messed-up families mean a messed-up church. Many well-meaning people are attempting to fix the church with programs and reforms. But you cannot fix the church unless you fix Dad. When you fix Dad, he reconnects the family. And reconnected families restore the church.

This is the program Christ used. He didn't try to change the Jewish nation from the top down. Instead, He worked with men, one individual heart at a time. He worked with Nicodemus; with the Roman Centurion; with Matthew, the tax collector; with Peter and Andrew, the fishermen; and even the demoniac who lived in the tombs of Decapolis. He worked to connect them with their only source of power—Himself. When they were connected to Him, their characters were transformed. And when their characters were transformed, they revolutionized their families, their communities, and even "turned the world upside down."[1]

This is how it works for us as well. Christ is seeking to draw each of us into a living connection with Him that will transform our thoughts, feelings, and habits to be like His. Thus empowered, we can become the guides for our families, leading, playing, talking, nurturing, correcting, and most of all, affirming them in the Way, the Truth, and the Life.

Mouse in the cookie jar

When it works at home, it will work anywhere. And when it is not working at home, don't fool yourself. You don't have genuine Christianity—regardless of your knowledge, zeal, or activity. I can't tell you the number of times I have met the children of leading ministers, their eyes downcast and miserable—"Dad has no time for me. He's too busy." We take this sad misrepresentation of Christianity that has alienated our children and try to sell it to the world.

We try eagerly to export our religion, but we have forgotten something. You see, the fact that a mouse is in the cookie jar doesn't make him a cookie. And just because we go to church and take our children to church and sit together as husbands and wives in church doesn't

---

1. Acts 17:6.

make us Christians. Christianity is about living the life of the Life-Giver. It is daily listening to our divine Coach and following His game plan in all the transactions of life. It's giving ourselves for our loved ones as Christ gave Himself for the church.

If this is truly our experience, why does the divorce rate of the church equal that of the world? Do we really have something to offer them? If so, why are our marriages in just as big a mess as theirs? How can we straighten out others' marriages when the marriages in our own churches are falling apart? Are we missing something?

ADDING AND SUBTRACTING

I believe our problem is that we have lost sight of gospel order. Gospel order is much like mathematics in that you must master the basics before you can hope to successfully tackle more complex operations. You must master addition and subtraction before you go on to multiplication and division.[2]

The addition and subtraction of Christianity is learning to cooperate with divine Grace.[3] Grace is given to everyone.[4] This means God is present in the life of every individual—wooing them, entreating them, beckoning them, trying to save them in the present, in the here and now. That does not make them a Christian. Every person—both Christian or otherwise—can trace God's hand in their lives if they take the time to look for it, but that does not mean they are saved. You can be loved and cared for by God and still be a mouse in the cookie jar.[5]

God is frustrated[6] when we go no further than merely enjoying the benefits of His blessings. We accept His grace as a gift and proudly parade the gift to others, telling them to get the gift too.[7] But God doesn't want us to just receive the gift. He wants us to open it.[8] When we open the gift of His grace, we find that it transforms us from a mouse to a cookie.[9]

---

2. See Luke 16:10.
3. See Matthew 6:33.
4. See Ephesians 4:7.
5. See Matthew 5:45.
6. See Galatians 2:21.
7. See 2 Corinthians 6:1.
8. See Ephesians 2:8–10.
9. See 1 Corinthians 5:17.

Our homes are both our testing ground and our school.[10] Our conduct in our homes reveals whether we are truly responding to divine grace or just fooling ourselves. Husbands will love their wives with the same self-sacrificing devotion that took Christ to the cross.[11] Fathers will give of their time, their ear, their interest to their children as our heavenly Father gives of Himself to His children.[12] The home will become a little heaven on earth because all is done decently and in order,[13] and faithfulness in the little things as well as the large becomes the norm.[14]

This is the adding and subtracting of Christianity. If you can't add and subtract, it doesn't matter how sincere you are. Your multiplication and division—your outreach and evangelism—will come out wrong. If a man fails to provide for the real needs of his family, he is not just a poor Christian, he is worse than an unbeliever.[15] Which is more disgusting? A mouse in the field or a mouse in the cookie jar?

Christianity must be lived in the home, which, I believe, is the hardest place for the Christian life to be lived. If you can't live it at home, don't try to give it to someone else. But when you can live it at home, you can live it anywhere. That's when it's time to export.

Jesus said, *This gospel* of the kingdom shall be preached in all the world."[16] Which gospel is He talking about? It is the gospel of His grace![17] It is the gospel that changes the mouse into a cookie! When you experience God's transforming power in your own life, you have something of real value to share.

The work of the ministry is simply sharing with families the gospel that *saved* and *is saving* me and my own family. It is teaching families how to live above the pull of their flesh. It is instructing them about

10. See Timothy 3:4, 5.
11. See Ephesians 5:25–33.
12. See Ephesians 6:4.
13. See 1 Corinthians 14:40.
14. See Luke 16:10.
15. See 1 Timothy 5:8.
16. See Matthew 24:14.
17. See Galatians 1:6.

God's beautiful truths and warning them of the enemy's clever counterfeits. Evangelism is merely accomplishing in others' lives what's been done in our own. It is simply applying to other marriages what has been applied in ours. It is pointing other families to what has worked in our family. That is gospel order.

How can we build up the church if we haven't built up our own marriages? How can we build up the community if we haven't built up our own families? We can't, friends. We simply cannot. No matter how successful our work for God outside the home *appears*, if our kind of Christianity still permits self to have its way and raise its ugly head on a regular basis—especially at home—it is not worth sending to the world. What we are giving to the world is in reality a misrepresentation, and it will mislead others, in spite of our sincerity.

I realize that some may think in saying this that I am against sending Christianity to the world. I am completely in favor of it. I believe the real question is not whether Christianity is worth exporting. Clearly it is. What we really need to ask ourselves is, Is *my kind* of Christianity—the kind I live behind closed doors with my family—worth exporting? That's the real question. Is our exporting motivated by a genuine outflowing of a daily walk with God, or has it become a substitute for Christ Himself and a convenient distraction to keep us from facing what we don't know how to deal with?

I know this is a disturbing thought because it disturbed me when I first faced it. I have found, though, that difficult questions often form the basis for deep personal growth in God. So don't shy away from them. Face them head-on.

A FRONT AND A FRAUD

I vividly remember a man who came to see me at a weekend retreat. He was not only a minister; he was a high-ranking church leader responsible for many churches, ministers, employees, and institutions. He sat down with me at a crowded lunch table, looked me straight in the eye, and said, "Jim, I'm a front and a fraud."

I was stunned, not so much at his words but at his candid admission. I searched his eyes and found honest misery. "Why do you say that?" I probed gently.

"When I'm visiting the churches, when I'm up in the pulpit, I look every bit the denominational leader. I play the part. I'm a front—what people expect to see. But . . ." he said, glancing at his wife beside him, "when I'm at home, I can't fake it, and my Christianity is a fraud." My eyes met his wife's eyes, and she just nodded sadly. Praise God for honest men, honest ministers, and honest church leaders who have the courage to look at themselves in the mirror and say, "I'm a fraud." God can work with men like that.

Men, we must seriously and honestly face this question: Am I a front and a fraud? Is *my* Christianity worth exporting? It is a vital issue for us all to consider, and it was precisely this type of introspection that motivated me to make hard yet vitally important changes in my life—changes that placed me in opposition to much of my fellow church members' conventional wisdom about outreach and ministry for others. It eventually revolutionized not only my personal understanding, but also my ministry.

THIRTY QUIET YEARS

This revolution began as I studied the life of Christ and began to ask, Why did Jesus spend thirty quiet years at home? I mean, how many sick people died that He could have healed? How many honest but ignorant hearts struggled through the years with their questions unsatisfied? How many widows buried their sons without the intervention of the Life-Giver? Why did He spend so much of His life doing the mundane chores of a carpenter while the needs of the world were so great? What was He doing? Was there a purpose to it all?

Over time, I began to recognize that His home was His training ground, just as my home was for me. He was trained by meeting the needs of His parents, the needs of His brothers and sisters, and the needs of His home. Of these years we know little other than that He grew in stature and in favor with God and man.

This period of quiet obscurity was His time of importing. Christ, our perfect Example, imported until the product was so good it was time to export. Oh, how I wish we would learn from His example! How little is ever said of the quiet years that fitted Him for the three and a half years of active ministry. Too often, we are so busy trying to copy the years of active ministry that we utterly miss the lessons of those early years, which make up the majority of His life. In fact, Jesus never forsook his home duties for a greater work. Even while He was dying on the cross, even while the fate of the entire world hung in the balances, even while He endured incomprehensible mental and physical suffering, He was concerned with the home duties. He gazed tenderly at the grief-stricken face of His mother, knowing she did not understand why He was allowing Himself to be killed. Gently, ever so gently, He reached out in one last act of love. "Mother, look at My beloved disciple, John. From now on, he will be your son and care for you." And to John He entreated, "Behold your mother."[18]

Amidst the greatest crisis the world has ever known, Jesus did not forget the home duties. He didn't say, "Mother, hang on until the crisis is over." He didn't excuse Himself, saying, "Mother, I'm sorry I can't deal with your problems right now—I'm carrying the fate of the whole world," or "The pain is too great to address your concerns." No, even when He was dying for your sins and mine, with Christ it was "family first." He spoke to John and "from that hour [John] took her unto his own home."[19]

Jesus didn't forget His mother, and that is what I refer to as gospel order—home first, then outreach. I meet so many men who have it backwards. We neglect our wives or our children for what we think is a greater work of witnessing and outreach, of church duties and responsibilities. Oh that every church would become established upon gospel order! We will never change the world until we do. If we embrace it as Christ did, we will become empowered to perform a mighty work in a very short time, just as Christ did in just three and a half years.

The real measure

However, it isn't always evangelism that men get caught up in. I've seen many men who neglected their first work at home because of their businesses or their own selfish interests or hobbies. Many of these men

---

18. See John 19:26, 27.
19. John 19:27.

are looked up to as leaders in their church and community, but your home life is the real measure of your manhood. Who you are at home is who you really are. The way you treat your spouse and children when no one else is looking is the real measure of your character. Our children, our families, and, to a lesser degree, those to whom we attempt to minister, reject the gospel not so much because they reject God but because of what they see or perhaps don't see in us. As Mahatma Gandhi once said, "I like your Christ. I do not like your Christians. Your Christians are so unlike your Christ."

Is this making you uncomfortable? If so, you are not alone. Many find this concept difficult to embrace because the implications are so life-changing in application. Bluntly stated, it "rocks the boat"! Let me explain. I was preaching in Europe on this very topic, saying that if our base camp—that is, our home—is in trouble, we don't belong on the front lines. Among the listeners was a very talented, sincere, zealous, young, and attractive couple who had thrown themselves wholeheartedly into the gospel ministry. At that time, they were conducting Bible studies in a dozen different homes! Everyone considered them highly effective workers and ardent Christians. But when the couple heard this simple yet profound perspective on gospel order, they decided they had a problem.

They told me afterwards, "Jim, we've put service before our Savior. We're exporting, when we haven't imported. We've been trying to save others drowning in sin, when we don't know how to swim ourselves. For example, we were on our way to one of our studies and all the way there we were fighting and bickering, yet when they answered the door we were all smiles, saying, 'Are you ready to learn more about the second coming of our Lord and Savior? Are you ready for Jesus to come?' We had a wonderful study, biblically accurate and uplifting. Then we got back in our car and picked up arguing and bickering with each other right where we had left off."

Is that how it is in your life? If a movie screen were to lower behind you as you sit in church, or preach, or give studies, or conduct your business, and a video featuring you as you behaved in your home this past week began to play, would you be at ease? Would your life practice match your profession?

BUTTERFLIES

This couple began to wake up. They began to realize that they had sincerely mistaken their duty. They remembered the words of Christ, " 'Not everyone who says to Me, "Lord, Lord," shall enter the kingdom of heaven, but he who *does* the will of My Father in heaven.' "[20] Notice, the text didn't mention anyone who "*knows* the will of My Father." It says anyone who "*does* the will of My Father." They discovered that their conversion to Christianity had been confined to doctrine and opinion. They had experienced an intellectual conversion rather than a heart conversion. Therefore their evangelism wasn't evangelism. It was what I call "churchianity" or "truthianity." It was introducing people to a church and a system of truth without connecting them to a living Savior.

This young couple looked at their life and concluded they had another work to tend to. In essence, they decided to admit that they were caterpillars and must enter into their cocoon in order to cooperate with God's transforming metamorphosis. When they could become "butterflies" at home, they could be "new creatures" anywhere. It's the difference between a caterpillar professing and pretending to be a butterfly and a caterpillar truly transformed into a butterfly. The genuine is much more convincing. Then they could encourage others that they too can change—that they don't have to crawl along on their bellies; that they can fly above the trials and temptations of daily life. They weren't selfish or critical of others; they had just caught a vision of a new and better way to minister, and they wanted to get their own wings.

Others didn't see it that way. They misunderstood this sincere couple's desires, and they got mad at me. Rumors came all the way back to me in Montana—"Don't invite Jim Hohnberger to speak in your churches. He's against outreach. He's opposed to evangelism!"

A MAVERICK

You know enough from reading this chapter that I'm not against outreach, but truth can never compete with rumor. What's true is that I am a maverick, trying to confront and combat an error that is robbing

---

20. Matthew 7:21, NKJV, italics added.

our churches of the real source of power. It is an error that at one time duped me, may be duping you, and has certainly duped many Christian churches and ministries.

I remember one man clearly. He was a naturally gifted and talented man. He had been successful in other fields before entering the gospel ministry. However, when I got acquainted with him, it became obvious that his marriage was a mess and his children were not in order. At least one son was living with a woman to whom he was not married. My heart ached for this sad situation, which is regrettably all too common among leading men.

Nevertheless I shared with him my understanding about gospel order and his need to import before he tried to export. He just shook his head at me, bewildered. "Jim, you're the only one who tells me I am unfit for the ministry. Everyone else says, 'We need your talents and abilities.' They see me as a reformer in the midst of a worldly church."

He was unwilling to reprioritize his life, and I sadly watched his ministry collapse some months later on the heels of his divorce. He isn't the only one suffering from the same delusion—believing that the importance of the work they are doing trumps their failures at home.

Base camp in order

Moses was prone to the same fallacy, but God stopped him in his tracks. Moses was setting out at God's command to deliver Israel from bondage when the angel of the Lord met him in the way with a threat to kill him. Why? Because Moses had neglected a known duty in his family. He had neglected to circumcise his son, and God would not allow him to continue his mission until he performed his duty.[21]

Men may not see home duties as very important, but in the end they determine the public ministry. Any general will tell you that the condition of your base camp determines the outcome of your campaign. Yet the devil tries continually to convince us that the rules don't apply to our unique circumstances. He tells us that the battles are too hard and the rewards too few. He exaggerates the obstacles and holds us in the mold passed on by generation after generation. Over and over, we fall

---

21. See Exodus 4:24.

for his lies and intimidations and remain locked in a stereotype that only produces heartache and failure.

It need not be so. God's plan of "family first" is simple and successful, and it will bring more sweetness into your life than you can imagine! It can be thus because Jesus has led the way and He knows the steps for us to take. If you will simply listen to His suggestions and follow His leading, you will begin to reap rewards that can't be compared with any other.

CHOCOLATE . . . CHOCOLATE . . . CHOCOLATE

The aroma of chocolate scented the air before we even opened the door. Sally looked at me, concern in her eyes. As we stepped into her mother's home, we saw chocolate candies of all imaginable varieties cooling on every possible surface of the kitchen, dining room, and living room.

Sally's mother greeted us warmly. "As you can see, I've been making candy today! I've had so much fun."

I started up the spiral staircase to put our two young boys to bed while Sally visited with her mother. I was nearing the top of the darkened stairs, when part of their conversation reached my ears. I glanced down toward the kitchen and saw Sally's mother holding a plate of tempting chocolates before Sally. "Go ahead," she was saying. "Jim will never know. These are your favorites!"

Sally's face was pale, and her eyes were filled with fear. You see, Sally had grown up in a home where her spirit was continually wounded and neglected and her basic emotional needs were almost never met. She learned to fill that vacuum for love with food—especially chocolate. Now that we had been in the mountains for some time, she was learning that God had better ways to meet her need for love than chocolate—and she was striving to overcome her addiction in that area. Do you or anyone you know struggle there? If so, you realize just how powerful are those impulses to indulge "just a little."

We had come back to Wisconsin to visit our families, and I offered to help the local pastor with visitation and Bible studies. We had scheduled the entire next day, and I knew he was counting on me. Sally and the boys would be spending time with her mother. That night and early in the morning as I talked with God, I wrestled in my mind. God was saying to me, *"Jim, will you get off your tractor and rescue Sally before this temptation sweeps her away? When your base camp is in trouble, you have no business going to the front lines."* You see, when my Sally is struggling under heavy temptation, my base camp is in trouble. I had already promised my time to the pastor. Didn't my previous commitment take precedence over my wife's personal struggles? Shouldn't she be able to deal with this on her own? Aren't those Bible studies more important than a "little thing" like chocolate?

At nine-thirty in the morning, there was a knock at the door. The pastor greeted me cheerily. "You ready to go, Jim?"

"Pastor, I'm really sorry, but I can't go with you today."

"What? I was really counting on you. What's up?"

"Well, pastor, when your base camp is in trouble, you don't belong on the front lines. My Sally is struggling with a major temptation, and I need to be here for her today. God has lain this very heavily on my heart, so I trust He will provide just what you need for your day also."

Sally overheard my conversation, and when I turned from the door, there were tears streaming down her lovely cheeks. "You're going to stay with me?"

"I'm here for you, dear. We'll face this thing together!"

And that's just what we did. When I saw the temptation in the house growing strong, the boys and I would take her to the park and play freeze tag. "Chase Mother, boys! Run hard and catch her." We worked through that day together, and Sally found freedom from the chocolate. She found it because my love for her made tangible God's love for her. The sparkle of victory in her eyes and the joy overflowing from her heart made my base camp a paradise!

Men, what are the tractors that occupy our time and attention while our loved ones cling to that slender willow branch, the muddy currents of life threatening to sweep them away? Let's not wait another moment. Let's all climb off those tractors now and get down into the canal to rescue our little Johnnies and Susies. Let's embrace that girl we married. Step by step, we can all get out of the ditch together!

Chapter 6
Family First

Questions to Consider for Personal Inventory or Group Discussion

1. What, in reality, is first in my life? What is second?
2. Where does my family truly come in on a daily basis?
3. How much undivided time and attention do I give them daily? Weekly?
4. Do I really know my children?
5. Is 1 Timothy 3:4, 5 a reality in my life?
6. What am I going to eliminate to make my family a priority?
7. Am I a front and a fraud?
8. If my family were to name me according to my most dominant characteristic, what would that be?
9. Why do I find it so-o-o hard to devote myself to them?
10. When will I begin to make them first?

"That's My Man"

"Yet there is one thing wrong; you don't love me as at first!
Think about those times of your first love (how different now!)
and turn back to me again and work as you did before."
—*Revelation 2:4, 5, TLB*

The tingling and burning sensation as my arm falls asleep distracts me. A rock is digging into my hip, and somewhere near my ankle an insect is taking advantage of the situation and crawling up my leg, tickling me. But these distractions are minor compared to the woman I'm with. I covertly flex my fingers, trying to urge some circulation back into my arm, so I can stay where I am a few more moments with Sally nestled up to me; for I am enjoying myself far too much for such minor inconveniences to interrupt me. I'm on a date with Sally.

I think back to that day in high school chemistry class when Sally walked into class and sat behind me. I knew then that there was something special about this girl! I'd dated other girls, and some I really liked, but there was more chemistry between Sally and me than there was in that chemistry class from the start, and it set our relationship apart from any others. I felt a special attraction from our very first date when she'd worn a blue and white striped shirt and white shorts. Such lovely memories!

Now as my arm ached, we lay together in the grassy clover, her head on my chest. As she studied the clouds, I studied her, and she talked and

102

talked and talked. It's not that I don't enjoy what she says, for certainly I do, but what I am finding pleasure in right now is the sound of her voice, marveling at her presence with me, admiring her simple, sweet beauty, and breathing in the wonderful perfume of her lovely hair. What a special girl she is!

BITTERSWEET MEMORIES

Do you remember when your love was like this—fresh, vibrant, and alive? When you lived simply to be with each other? I think most of us do, and yet almost all of us have suffered from the slow erosion process that steals our first love experience. Blissful memories of our special times fade into yesteryear, and we wonder if they will ever come again— maybe in retirement, we speculate, or perhaps that is just the way things go.

It has been a bittersweet experience for me to explore the joys of my courtship with Sally and how we allowed them to escape us over the years. I discovered, in this process, some keys to rekindling the flame of love in my marriage. Because I have talked with many hundreds of men about their marriages, I know there is a good chance that you share the same tendencies I have to take my wife for granted, to become too busy, to allow my love to grow cold, or to treat her as a convenience. So I am not going to beat you up for things you did or didn't do. I was in the same boat, and perhaps there is some benefit in sharing more of my experiences with Sally; for we have traveled the road you are on.

WINNING HER HEART

My girl, Sally, was complicated. She came from such a different, difficult, and complex family background that I could hardly comprehend her struggles and had no reference point for her experiences. Yet, every time we walked through a meadow or sat on a rocky outcrop, she'd share a little bit and then watch to see how I'd respond. For a long time, her timidity and fear of rejection kept her conversation general. But when I encouraged her questions and appreciated her thoughts, she was able to relax, open up, and be herself. I was just a teenager, but I listened compassionately, sharing my understanding and sympathy. When I thought I had something useful, I'd offer her solutions. The more she shared with me and met with acceptance, the more she trusted me. Soon I became the confidant. I listened to her hurts, her joys, her dreams, and her disappointments. I learned early on that with this complex and alluring girl, I had to dig for her meanings on everything and evaluate what she meant, rather than what she'd actually said. I discovered she didn't communicate the same way I did, and it had nothing to do with intelligence or ability but rather with the unique way in which she expressed herself as a woman.

Soon we were inseparable. We found ourselves traveling life's road side by side as true companions.

Now you know what I did for Sally, but let me tell you what she did for me, and it wasn't complicated. She treated me like a king, and I loved it. I couldn't imagine anyone else I'd rather spend time with. Back in those days, when your interests centered on one and only one person, we called it going steady. I don't know what they call it now. Going out with Sally was pure bliss, and we began seeing each other exclusively without even talking about it.

LOVE OF MY LIFE!

I talked so much more in depth with Sally than I had with any woman, and I soon found myself attracted to her heart and character, as well as her good looks. She had her own personality and cute way of communicating. She wasn't like so many girls—phony, stuck-up, or wimpy when it came to climbing cliffs or jumping over creeks and rocks. She loved a good time as much as I did and was willing to take chances and put forth effort in our recreation. She became the apple of my eye, and nothing was too difficult for me to do for the one I loved.

I showered her with affection and attention. I looked for things to compliment her on. I'd do little things for her—wash her car, fix her mother's roof, and even help with the dishes because anything was a joy with "My Love". I'm not sure I've ever been so consistently considerate in all my life. I mean, I opened the door for her *every* single time. I helped with her coat. If she forgot something—no big deal—we went back for it. If she said something wrong, I laughed it off. If she needed help, I came over. If she made a mistake, it was erased from my mind instantly. There was no sensitivity, kindness, or gentleness I wouldn't exert for Sally because *I was in love with her*. Sure, there was a downside to Sally—nearly everyone has one. But it seemed so minor, so insignificant compared to the upside.

As Sally experienced these attentions consistently day in and day out, she was swept off her feet. I was Mr. Considerate, and Sally thought, *That's my man. He's going to take care of me, meet my needs, and respect my ideas. He's my protector, my provider, and the love of my life! He treasures me. He encourages me. He'll do anything for me. I've never been so loved, so cherished in my whole life. Yes, I'd gladly marry this guy!*

IRRESISTIBLE!

The more time I spent with Sally, the more I found her irresistible. I willingly gave up all my former joys and pleasures to be with her. When we were in college separated by many miles, I gladly sacrificed time with my buddies, my football games, my hunting. I'd give up anything that stood in the way of seeing Sally.

One weekend a terrible snowstorm with howling winds and drifts closed the roads. Sally knew we were supposed to get together, but it looked impossible. No one could travel. The police had shut the highways. Nothing could get through . . . but I showed up. Pursuing Sally had become my pleasure and my focus. She had become the priority of my life, and I could deny myself any pleasure—except being with her. Long before we were married, we had become one in spirit. We left on our honeymoon knowing we were going to live happily ever after—just like all the fairy tales said, and for a time our marriage really was this way.

INNOCENT BEGINNINGS

Upon graduation from college, we went back to our hometown and bought a brand-new house. I wish you could have seen our little home. It was entirely empty except for a used bedroom set! We didn't even own a refrigerator or a stove! We had a Coleman cooler and a Weber grill, and we'd eat on the back steps or lounge on the carpet in the living room, imagining the day we'd buy our dream furnishings. We talked, laughed, flirted, and chased each other about like kids. Our home was full of love, fun, and companionship. Our experience was sweet with our innocent faith that we were going to make it.

And then *life* intruded.

My work sent me for training in New York for thirty days. Sally and I had never spent this long apart, even in college. I was determined to be a good provider, and if this was what it required, I'd do it and we'd survive.

THE EROSION BEGINS

I didn't think about it at the time, but this was the first time since we began dating that I had valued anything over and above Sally. I thought I was doing it for Sally. This is so typical of the devil's distractions and temptations, making them look so good, so helpful, and so necessary. Sally and I bought into this idea of sacrificing our relationship to get ahead in business, and by the time I returned thirty days later, I found an empty house. Sally was working from three in the afternoon until eleven at night as an RN at the hospital, and I came home every evening to a lonely, empty house. To fill the void, I threw myself into sports such as hunting and racquetball and started going out with the guys.

Sally would come home when my day was long over and still be sleeping when I left for work in the morning. She woke up to an empty house and felt just as isolated and lonely as I did. She had to fill her time now that I was increasingly unavailable, so she hung out with her friends, shopped, and did crafts. Both of us had started out with a sincere longing to spend time with each other, but somehow the busyness of life became more important than being with each other. Our hard work eventually brought financial success, and with it came a new and bigger home (furnished this time), new cars, and then another upgraded home. My business thrived, and the weeks grew into months and then years as we built wealth.

DISPLACED

I found that worldly success eclipsed Sally as irresistible. I still loved her honestly and sincerely, but I wasn't "in love" with her. She was no longer number one on my list. With my attentions waning, Sally experienced the same type of change in her feelings. She went from being in love and feeling like the most cherished woman on earth—literally on top of the world—to being just convenient and familiar. If I could have read her feelings at this point they wouldn't have been saying, "That's my man." They would have said, "That *was* my man. Oh how I loved him and wish he was the way he used to be."

Rosemary, one of Sally's friends, told us the story of her twenty-fifth wedding anniversary. Her husband was a successful man, and together they made an intelligent, articulate couple with a big, beautiful home that Sally and I could only admire and aspire to one day in the future. The weekend of their anniversary her husband was gone on a fishing trip with his buddies, but she wasn't worried. She knew he'd be back for their anniversary.

But he didn't show up. He sent two dozen roses instead.

When he returned a day later he found the roses shredded and tossed in the trashcan. Their confrontation was sharp. "You care more about the opening day of fishing with your buddies than you do about me!"

He was taken aback. "Rosemary, I don't understand. I usually send you a dozen roses on our anniversary, but because I was gone I sent two to make up the difference." He just didn't get it. He didn't grasp that a woman cannot feel cherished when she holds less interest for him than the opening day of fishing . . . or his business . . . or the Internet . . . or anything else. Twenty dozen roses would not have made up for the lack of his presence. Nothing can replace the heart of a husband truly cherishing his wife.

NOT ME!

Not long after Sally shared with me Rosemary's story, we joined another couple and their teenage son for a weekend hike and picnic. Rita had carefully planned a sumptuous picnic for their family and loaded the daypack, and Sally had done the same for us. We met at the trailhead, and Sally and Rita went to use the facilities. While they were gone, Troy, their teenage son, eyed the large daypack and asked his father, "Are you going to carry the pack?"

"No," he replied. "Mother packed it; let her carry it!" And seeing his wife returning from the bathroom, he turned and walked down the trail ahead of us all. I was embarrassed for them and busied myself with my own daypack.

"Mom, I don't understand Dad's attitude," Troy said, puzzled as he shouldered the pack himself. "Why is he so selfish?"

"Son, your father lost interest in me years ago. He sees only his needs. Selfishness all too easily replaces love." And smiling at us to ease the awkwardness, she led the way down the trail after him.

I was shocked and saddened. Confident I would never do anything stupid like that, I was blissfully unaware that I was already far down the pathway of ignoring Sally.

During this time we'd become Bible-believing Christians, but this didn't transform our marriage. All my Bible study and scholarship didn't change me back to the attentive man who had once single-mindedly sought Sally's love and affection. Now I was a stressed-out business owner, a distant husband, and a father who demanded his needs be met while ignoring his wife's burdens. I had become a man proud of my spiritual knowledge but devoid of true spiritual transformation, pretending to everyone, even myself, that I was a Christian. The problem was that I couldn't fool Sally—she lived with me. She knew the real state of my spiritual life. Even worse was the fact that in her own spiritual journey there had been born in her heart the desire for her husband to become the spiritual leader in the home. Yikes—that's me! It wasn't that I didn't want to, but I just had no idea how to accomplish it. I didn't think I could do it.

TURNING POINT

A crazy fight over hash browns brought things to a head. As Sally and I talked and talked, really communicating for the first time in years, we realized we had been happier back in our empty house when we had absolutely nothing and were in love with each other than now that we had everything money could buy. For us, it was a moment of decision. Would we continue down the path we were on and end up divorced or estranged or just co-habiting together? Or would we turn about-face? We decided to reorder our lives. What we really wanted was to be living, breathing Christians. We wanted our home to demonstrate Christianity in action, not just in name. We wanted to be "in love" once more and have our marriage achieve all the promise it had held at our beginning. To do this, we concluded we'd sell everything and move off to the wilderness, but we arrived there with a marriage in need of serious rehabilitation.

COMMITTED BUT CLUELESS

It was almost overwhelming to face what we faced when we settled into our little log cabin. We were committed to repairing our family as well as our marriage, but we were clueless about where to begin. We knew somehow that the key was finding an authentic walk with God, but it felt like we were groping in the dark. Gradually we learned that God wanted to be more than Someone we worshiped, more than even a Friend we communed with morning and evening, but a constant Guide throughout the day—each and every moment of the day.

When I caught this vision, I knew I wanted the experience. So I tried it and fell flat on my face. I tried it over and over with the same dismal result, and then I experienced a few small successes that encouraged me to continue onward and upward. I share this because if you desire to transform your life with God, you will likely experience this same pattern. It happens not because God preordains our failure but because our old habits of responding without thinking are so deeply ingrained. It takes a lot of practice to learn not only to think before we act or speak but also to ask God what we should do in every situation. It sometimes takes those repeated failures to teach us how to distrust our own wisdom and put confidence in His wisdom and knowledge. God isn't as concerned with our failures as He is with what we do with them. Do we go to Him to learn from our bungled attempts to love our wives? Do we get back up and try again? That's what He's interested in because He knows that if we don't give up, we will eventually find success—and that success will breed more success.

I did find a few things aided me in this struggle. The most important was control over my time. By changing our lifestyle and bringing life down to the irreducible minimum, I lowered the cost of living, and this meant I had to work less. Thus, I had more time I could invest in my family—in my marriage.

Rekindling

I began to do all the old things I used to do when we were in love. However, I discovered that what you do when you are in love is easy. What you do when you love but are no longer "in love" is much harder because there is no wave of good feelings as a catalyst to self-denial. I started doing things the way I had when we dated, and I wondered why Sally didn't respond more—after all, I was doing what she wanted, wasn't I? I came to realize that Sally is pretty smart. She was waiting to see if I was going to be constant and trustworthy. She had thought I was Mr. Perfect before, when we were dating, and found after she was married that I wasn't quite so great. Your wife may watch and wait a while to see if you've really changed. The best policy is to do what God is asking of you and not worry about the results. Leave them entirely to God.

Never too late!

Now some of the husbands I have counseled don't have a storybook courtship with their wives to refer back to. Lust, insecurity, or some other emotional baggage drove their attraction to each other. Is their case hopeless? Not at all! I have heard it said that with Christ, it is never too late to have a happy childhood. The same holds true for courtship. With Christ, it is never too late to apply His principles to your marriage. When we men begin to focus on what God would have us think, feel, say, and do with our wives rather than what our past has programmed us to do, we can experience heaven on earth for the first time.

The key is seeking to understand what makes your wife feel unloved and stop doing that and, at the same time, to discern what makes her feel cherished and start doing that. You will probably find, like me, that the self-denial required penetrates deep and you will feel at first like you fail more times than you win. But if you keep coming back to God and trying what He suggests to you, your successes will eventually outnumber your bloopers.

Irresistible again

Guess what, guys! It works! I know—it worked for me! But it worked backwards. I thought my actions were going to rekindle her love toward me, but instead they rekindled my love for her, which in turn relit the flame of love in her heart. When I treated her as if she was irresistible, she gradually became irresistible once more. The spark returned to our love. We started having fun together. Once more we flirted and played. This was not just a physical pursuit but a falling in love with her, with who Sally is—her personality, her character, and her thoughts. I realize now, much more than back then, that this means far more to a woman than just desire for her physically. A woman wants to be loved, truly loved and cherished, for who she is. This kindles the responding chord of admiration toward her husband, awakens friendship and trust, allowing her to love once more. It works, gentlemen—it works! I wanted to shout from the housetop—we were in love once more. It really could happen again. God worked this miracle in my life, and I know He can do it in yours.

That's my man!

A sudden sharp pain near my ankle jerks me upright to swat a pesky fly away and displaces Sally.

"You've been awfully quiet while we've been lying here," she comments. "Whatcha been thinking?"

"About you . . . us, I mean. How things used to be and how much better they are now."

She smiled impishly. "I wondered what was on your mind when you asked me out on a date in the middle of the day. You're just as mischievous now as you ever were."

"Oh, and you're not? Why are you grinning like the cat that ate the canary?"

"I'm thinking about the meal I left for us in the warming oven." She met my eyes shyly and continued, "I made all your favorites."

"And something special for dessert?" I inquired teasingly.

"You'll just have to wait and see," she said, jumping to her feet. "You might have to catch me to find out!" she shouted over her shoulder as she ran for the house.

It all sounded wonderful, but Sally, that rascal, had intentionally caught me with my shoes off, giving her a big head start. At last I bounded after her, our laughter spilling over the wilderness. I didn't capture my vision of loveliness until I burst into the dining room, breathless but happy, and enclosed her in my arms with an affectionate kiss.

The table is set, and the food is more tempting than that of the finest restaurant. I look at Sally, the girl I have loved for all these years, and marvel inwardly that in my life today, not just when we were dating, the fires of love are still burning brightly. She glows with love and joy, a blossoming, fulfilled woman. Face to face, we hold our embrace for just a moment longer. She snuggles in close to my chest, breathing out a sigh of contentment as she whispers, "That's my man!"

CHAPTER 7
"THAT'S MY MAN"
Questions to Consider for Personal Inventory or Group Discussion

1. Have I lost the joys of my courtship with my wife?
2. Would my wife now say, "That's my man" or would she say, "That *was* my man"?
3. On an "A-B-C-D-F" scale, how would my wife rate me?
4. What has displaced my wife from being number one in my thoughts and time?
5. Do I truly love my wife more than my job, my sports, my buddies, or my outreach?
6. Do I sacrifice for my wife daily?
7. When was the last time I took my wife's hand and went for a walk?
8. When was the last time I went on a date with my wife?
9. When was the last time I really listened to her—to know what is going on in her heart?
10. What would it take to rekindle my love?
11. Will I map out a course to "re-fall in love" with my wife and stick to it?
12. Will I treat her like a queen every day?
13. As the Spirit impresses, will I give her little attentions often?

Intimacy: The Byproduct

When Phil came to see me, I knew at first glance that he was a man accustomed to achievement. He strode confidently toward me, his trim, well-developed physique conveying strength and vitality beneath expensive casual clothing. Only the gray hair at the temples and the discerning scrutiny in his eyes belied his middle age. I soon learned he was a successful entrepreneur, owning a succession of businesses, always selling them at a substantial profit. Yet it was clear as we got to know one another that something was really troubling him, and it didn't take long for the problem to surface.

"Jim, I . . . we . . . er, well I mean . . . my wife needs counseling."

No wife was present, but I asked, "What is the matter?"

"When we were first married she was very affectionate, loving, and our love was passionate and physical."

"How did you feel about her then?"

"I was so in love, I hardly knew when my feet hit the ground and physically, well, you haven't met her yet—when you do, you'll understand. She's beautiful, Jim. I couldn't resist her and never even tried." A look of sadness suddenly clouded his face, and the enthusiasm drained from his eyes as he ruefully shook his head. "Now she's cold, reserved, undemonstrative, and quite frankly, unavailable."

"So you're telling me at one time you two enjoyed a fantastic love life and that you shared true intimacy—not just physical union, and you really connected with each other on many levels?"

"That's it, Jim! It was so wonderful, so fulfilling, and now it has gone so terribly wrong. Could you talk to Sherry . . . you know, get her to change?"

"Would she talk with me?"

"Yes, I think she would."

"All right, how about we meet together tomorrow afternoon?"

"That would be great!"

"Phil, I want you to understand that I am not going into this meeting as your advocate nor as your adversary. I'll simply ask questions or make suggestions based upon my experience with many other couples, my own marriage, and most important, my understanding of the Holy Spirit's leading. I am looking for God-inspired solutions, and I know God desires for you and Sherry to have a fantastic relationship on every level. However, His solutions are not always the ones we expect."

"Don't worry about us, Jim. Sherry and I both want things to get better. We just can't seem to be able to turn things around by ourselves."

Opening it up

The next afternoon the three of us went for a walk together. I explained to both of them that we were seeking solutions, and while problems might be mentioned, they were being brought up only in the context of seeking solutions. "I do not need very long to understand your problems, so if you begin to bring them up more than once I will remind you that we are here seeking solutions." By this time we were walking down a lovely country lane, the sunshine reflecting off the grasshoppers that leaped away at our passing into the lustrous green meadow that lay by the roadside. Delicate wildflowers and an old stone fence graced the meadow. Nature seemed to be trying its best to convey the peace and love of its Creator toward Phil and Sherry. But the conflict that lurked beneath the surface of their lives seemed to make them oblivious to the glorious afternoon.

"Sherry," I began, "Phil tells me the two of you are experiencing a problem with intimacy, that you are cold and unresponsive to him." She turned to face me, bristling with hostility, and it was not hard to read her eyes. They plainly said, "Watch it, mister! You don't know what's going on between us, and if you step over the line and side with him there's going to be trouble between us!"

At that moment I wished she knew how much I empathized with her, that I was her ally seeking a solution, not her adversary to condemn her and yet, I couldn't start gently. I had to be direct. Too much water had gone under the bridge of their marriage. Too many times they'd suppressed their feelings and thoughts and pretended things were OK when they weren't. Too many times this dear woman had opened herself up to find a solution, only to be hurt and rejected. Something had to be different this time. I sensed God was leading in my approach. I searched her face for clues and realized her hostile expression was really a mask to hide her sadness and hurt—a protective measure holding her vulnerability in check. She needed just a little prompting for the truth to all come out. So with a prayer in my heart, I proceeded. "Sherry, is this true? Are you unresponsive, distant, and cold to Phil?"

"Yes! Yes I'm cold!" she blurted out, the pain evident in her expression. The next moment it changed, as the humiliation of being considered inadequate washed over her face. I waited as her emotions changed again. Anger followed, as it usually does. Experience has taught me that anger will normally boil to the surface and with it the truth, and in this, Sherry was no exception.

"You'd be cold too if he treated you the way he treats me! Do you really want to know why I'm cold?" There was a challenge in her face as if to say, "I double-dare you to ask me for the real story." It was exactly what I had been hoping and praying for.

"Absolutely! You take as much time as you want. Phil and I won't interrupt. You tell me exactly how things got the way they are." I glanced at Phil and noticed he wasn't so composed now.

"From the beginning?"

"Wherever you want to start will be just fine."

HER SIDE

"We've been together a lot of years, Mr. Hohnberger, a lot of years. When we were dating it was—like a fairy tale or something. I mean, he was my prince come to take me away to live happily ever after. He treated me better than anyone, and I mean anyone, had ever treated me. He respected me. He cared about my ideas, my goals, even my silly little dreams. I could be myself around him and he still loved me. I was so happy." Tears ran down her cheeks as she continued. "On our honeymoon, it was sheer joy. Afterwards, I lived for the moments we could be together. I didn't require anything except him, and it all slipped away from me," she said bitterly, amid sobs.

"He used to encourage me no matter what I attempted; he was my strength, always supporting me. I could do no wrong in his eyes. He thought I was perfect. I knew better, but it was so lovely to be so cherished." She paused to blow her nose and dab at her tears. "But all that is years ago. Now I only hear criticism and complaints. He blows up if I don't think, act, or react the way he thinks I ought to. He's a busy and successful man, and we live an affluent life, but he never seems to have time to fix things around the house or to spend time with the kids. Then when I risk a blowup to encourage him to spend time with me, or at least the children, he agrees, but never does it. I can't tell you how demeaning it feels to go from being number one on his list to somewhere below the evening news or surfing the Web on the computer. I'd like to take a hammer to that thing. It's like his computer is the other woman—stealing my husband from my family and me.

"Oh yes, he brings me flowers on my birthday or anniversary, but his lack of attention the rest of the year makes me feel like I'm going out on a blind date when I'm with him—not that we even go out anymore. Sure we get pizza or fast food when we don't have time to cook or we're traveling, but I can't remember the last time we ate out, just the two of us, in a romantic setting. And speaking of romance, he has the nerve to tell you I'm not interested. I'd be interested with the right man. I've got wants, needs, and desires, just like any other woman, but let me tell you, I sometimes go days without an adult conversation. He used to love to talk with me, to hold my hand while we walked or drove and to hug me for no reason at all."

"When I try to hug you, you stiffen up like a board," Phil interjected defensively.

"Please, let Sherry tell it her way," I reminded him.

"I do stiffen when you try to hug me because nowadays the only time you give me a hug is as a prelude to heading for the bedroom. We hardly know one another anymore, and you want me to respond to you after you ignored or mistreated me all week? I can't and I won't! I refuse to cheapen what's left of my self-esteem by engaging in an activity that is not reflected in the rest of our relationship. I am not a prostitute. I'd willingly give myself to the man I love, but he has gone somewhere and I can't find him anymore," she lamented, her voice breaking. After a moment, she wiped her eyes with the back of her hand and continued. "I refuse to make love anymore when I am not loved or don't feel loved. Mr. Hohnberger, I have been faithful to my marriage vows, but I can't continue to go the direction things are headed."

WHERE DO WE GO NOW?

The fire was out of her now and while her words had been hostile at times, I sensed in her bitterness the awful ring of truth. "Phil, has Sherry shared the way things go in your house?"

"Well, not exactly, Jim," he said, squirming. "She exaggerated some of the details."

"Phil, aside from a few disputed details, is everything *about* like she described?"

"Perhaps, sort of," he mumbled, refusing to look at me.

The ball was clearly in my court now. They both were awaiting my pronouncement. "Sherry, I want to tell you something. I don't blame you for being unresponsive, not at all, and as long as Phil continues to treat you the way he has been, I wouldn't share intimacy with him either!"

Her face brightened. You could easily read her thoughts. *You mean I am not going to get a lecture about my wifely duties? You mean my concerns are valid? You mean I am justified to feel the way I do?*

"Sherry, I don't think I need to talk with you any longer. If you wouldn't mind excusing us, I believe Phil and I need to continue *our* conversation." She looked at me and smiled. Phil had been right about one thing; she was really quite beautiful when she wasn't in tears. With a meaningful glance at Phil, Sherry left him to his fate and walked back down the road.

THE CRUX OF THE ISSUE

Phil sank onto a large rock nearby. "Jim, that wasn't exactly what I had in mind when I asked you to talk to my wife about our lack of intimacy."

"Be honest, Phil. Did you really want me to try some humanistic method to coerce her into behaving the way you think she ought to? I don't have any magical powers to turn your relationship around, but you do! She still wants to love you, still does love you deep down, but it is as certain as a mathematical equation—no intimacy all day equals no intimacy at night."

"Jim, I don't know, don't even understand why I react the way I do sometimes. She says something and before I even know it, I am yelling at her. I can't seem to stop."

"Phil, have you ever worked for someone else? Ever had a boss?"

"Sure, we all have at one time or another."

"Did he or she ever say things that irritated you, really irked you and made you mad?"

"Yeah, I worked for this one guy. He was a real jerk—so narrow-minded it wasn't funny. There was only one way, his way, and I made the mistake of trying to streamline the ordering process for our customers. He had an absolute tantrum. I was right and everyone except the boss knew it. He told me off in front of a room full of my co-workers and left me feeling an inch high."

"What did you do? Did you yell at him?"

"I needed that job and paycheck, so I bit my tongue, but let me tell you . . . as soon as I could, I left and found a better job."

"Don't you think you need an affectionate spouse at least as much as a paycheck?"

He got the strangest look on his face and then laughed out loud. "I guess I've been a fool."

"No, just human . . . like the rest of us. You see, Phil, selfishness comes naturally to all of us. It is the very nature we are born with. God provides us with the opportunity to change all that and to become empowered by Him so that we no longer respond automatically to our flesh and yell at our wives, so that we stop treating them as last on our list. If you are willing to do this God's way, you will be shocked at how readily she not only forgives but also responds to you once more.

"Real intimacy between a man and woman comes from admiration of the other individual. As we lose ourselves in admiration, we express it in many, many ways. We find ourselves amazed that such a wonderful being desires to be with us and cares about us. We find no effort too great to put forth if it will please them.

A SIMPLE SOLUTION

"Phil, you are going to have to court her once more. She needs to see you listening to your divine Coach, coming under His guidance, and restraining your temper. She needs to experience you filtering all you do and say through God. As you do this, He will provide you with ideas of how to reach her heart, and as you implement them, she will be convinced that you are genuinely interested in her as a friend—not for what you can get out of her, but for the lovely individual she truly is. When she sees you putting forth effort—real effort—to deny yourself for her sake, then and only then will she feel loved once more. When you do this she will once again respect you and open back up her love for you and you will be restored to your position at the center of her affections.

"Under this type of divine guidance, Sherry will become your focus, time with her your goal, and conversation with her more fulfilling than with anyone else. As God draws your hearts together in mutual admiration, a love that is greater than the sum of its parts will grow between you. This is exactly how God designed it to be. Physical intimacy is just the ultimate expression of such a process, and God rejoices in sharing with us such a wonderful tool to bind our hearts together in a trusting and mutually caring act.

CRITICAL CHANGES UNDETECTED

"However, what has happened in far too many of our relationships is that we have lost some of those special qualities that our wives once admired. Instead of a man they are in love with, we become a man they are concerned about. Often they don't know how to express their concerns, and just as often, we aren't willing to deal with them and resolve difficulties honestly. Thus resentment flows like a fast-moving stream that erodes and undercuts the steep, soft bank of intimacy. Like a precarious stream bank, we may not notice how bad the situation has become until the bank collapses and dumps us into the waters of marital crisis.

"Phil, like most men, your failure to honestly hear and deal with her legitimate concerns makes you less of a real man in her eyes, and when she loses respect for you, you can be certain that problems with intimacy will follow."

"Can I get her back?"

"You can, but it depends upon your willingness to change your focus from trying to get what you want to becoming a man she can admire—one she not only loves but also to whom she loves to give herself because she is loved and appreciated. I know, Phil, because my marriage was not always what it is today.

"For years Sally had tried to visit with me, talk about her troubles and trials, and I always brushed her concerns aside as unimportant, silly, or just plain foolish. But after we moved to the wilderness I got a rude awakening when I found out that every one of those burdens she had tried to share with me had not disappeared but had simply been stuffed down and tucked away. When I was at last ready to deal with her honestly and really *hear* what she was saying, I had a lot of past problems to deal with. I discovered that for Sally, my time and my affirming words toward her were more important than anything else. And there was a reason. I showed I cared by listening and hearing what she had to say and by not tuning her out. When I tuned out she knew it, and the message she got was that she wasn't worth hearing—that she was dumb and stupid—and why would she want to be intimate with someone who saw her that way? Only as she was heard, valued, and appreciated did she feel loved and cherished. When she felt loved, intimacy was an easy byproduct. I must confess that I had a much larger learning curve than Sally did in meeting my partner's needs. For you see, from the start Sally had intuitively understood that I responded best to loving acts of service, and she had done a wonderful job of meeting my needs.

"Now every person is different, and what matters to Sally or to me may not matter to you or your spouse. What is certain is that everyone has special things they respond to. Sometimes it's gifts, sometimes just uninterrupted time. For others it may be the tender touches of love or a combination of things. Phil, you know your wife. What did you do when you were courting her that she loved?"

RESTORING ROMANCE

"Jim, when we were dating we didn't have much money and we lived near the shore, so we used to walk barefoot on the sand for miles and talk of our plans and dreams. She was the most wonderful, most perfect woman I had ever known. I was working and going to college then, and I often wasn't available until sundown, but those summer nights were warm, and she'd pack us special meals of fresh fruits and sandwiches, and we'd picnic in the moonlight on the deserted beach with the sounds of the surf and a million stars overhead. We shared our first kiss under a full July moon as the waves washed about our toes."

"When was the last time you two shared like that, kissed on a moonlit beach, or walked for hours just enjoying the sound of her voice?"

"I can't remember. With the kids and my businesses we don't have time for such things anymore. I mean, it happens to all couples, doesn't it? The honeymoon is over and you pick up the burdens of adult life."

"Have you enjoyed life the way you are living now or would you go back to the time before you were wealthy?"

"I'd trade back in a minute if I could."

"What about your wife?"

"I know she hates the hours I work. Even when I sold off a business, I always had a new one, sometimes more than one before the old business sold. She has everything money can buy, but she isn't happy."

"That's because money can't buy you."

"You really think so?" Phil asked, his face brightening.

"Absolutely! You take the time to begin courting her once more, and your marriage is going to improve. Your businesses steal time from her, and she resents them because they rob her of you. If you choose to surrender to God and allow Him to guide your renewed courtship, not only is your marriage going to improve, but also you are going to experience a little taste of heaven."

A STEP IN THE RIGHT DIRECTION

"Thanks, Jim! I bet you don't get too many cases like mine to deal with, do you?"

"Actually, Phil, the number one reason men seek counseling with me is not spiritual guidance; it is not to find out how to be a better husband or father; nor is it to discuss their plans for country living or a career change. No, the number one reason men seek out my counsel is a lack of intimacy in their marriage."

Phil shook his head in amazement, but I continued, "I know you understand the courage it takes to seek counsel for this problem, but what you don't know is how my heart rejoices that God led you and many other men to *seek* counsel. This experience, while sometimes difficult—"

"You can say that again!" Phil interjected. "And embarrassing."

"Yes, it's hard, but it demonstrates that God has been preparing your heart for some significant changes, and if you are willing to cooperate with God, your experience of intimacy, as expressed in the marriage relationship, is about to undergo a radical change for the better."

LISTEN UP!

After I left Phil, I thought back to some letters I had received recently. In my quest to understand and help those who struggle with intimacy, I asked some of the women I know to write their husbands a letter talking about their marriage and why they didn't want to be intimate. I had no idea how poignantly eloquent these hurting women could be. I also found that while they would write the letter and share it with me, they were often too worried about their husband's reactions to even begin to share it with him. To me, this speaks volumes about how far down the wrong pathway many marriages have traveled.

One woman wrote the following letter:

I remember our brief courtship with a mingling of fondness and sadness—fondness at the way you wooed me and sadness at how quickly it vanished after our marriage. You told me how you felt you had found a treasure in me and your actions told me nothing was too good for me. I, in turn, thought I had found in you someone who'd listen to me, understand and care about me. We planned together to make communication a priority and vowed not to allow hurt feelings to go uncared for. You promised you would share all of life's burdens including the home duties.

These things all slipped away shortly after our honeymoon and I became a commodity, expected to play a certain role in your life. All of a sudden communications soured, hurt feelings no longer mattered, as you displayed a moodiness and irritation I had never seen in our courtship. You complained bitterly that you resented being expected to help in the home duties and I soon learned that you expected me to carry whatever burdens you didn't want to carry including the emotional load of the marriage. I was expected to not only satisfy your needs, but to anticipate them, all the while having no needs of my own.

I was not allowed to have my own feelings or ideas unless they did not conflict with yours. I often had deep misgivings as I saw you treat bank tellers and cashiers with more thoughtfulness than I received, as your wife. Deeply insecure, I craved acceptance from you and the only time I could depend upon a tender response from you was in our lovemaking. It seemed the only way I could gain a measure of acceptance from you was to try to satisfy you physically and my emotional needs led me to establish few boundaries with you in this area. But while you seemed happy I was in increasingly deep emotional pain because our marriage seemed based upon little more than our sexual relationship and this intimacy all on its own was so superficial.

Then everything changed with my pregnancy and miscarriage. Emotionally drained, I no longer had the capacity to satisfy you physically and my one area of acceptance became a touchstone of demand and scorn. It isn't that I didn't try. I did everything I could think of from self-help books to testosterone. I tried just gritting my teeth and doing it, but nothing worked and at last I realized that I couldn't satisfy you enough physically—no human female could satisfy you enough physically—so that you'd become a thoughtful, sensitive human being.

This failure drove me to God and I found many ideas I had held about Him were misguided. I began to test God personally and found He was not interested in the role I could play, but that He loved me. Rather than scorning me because of the deep hurts and festering wounds of my heart He drew me nearer to Him and as I began to give myself unreservedly to Him, I found my craving for love and acceptance satisfied. I have learned that I can be a happy person and wife even though I have a miserable marriage.

I no longer find the need to get some sort of emotional fix from satisfying you physically and our attempts these days leave me feeling dirty and used. How can you treat me as your worst enemy during the day or worse, simply ignore me as a person, and then expect me to enter enthusiastically into lovemaking at night? This is something I cannot comprehend and it fills me with revulsion.

I beg of you to drop your focus upon the physical and learn of Jesus how to be a savior in our home. I long for you to find Jesus in a way that would transform your character and enable us to be true companions. I long for our "one-flesh" experience to be an outgrowth of our "one-heart" experience in God—not a cheap substitute for it. While you give lip service to this idea, you have not pursued it whole-heartedly. Please learn of God how to be consistently attentive, gentle, and considerate. Allow Him to bind our hearts together with His unselfish love. Let Him restore the lost joys of our courtship. My heart was once yours—it can be yours again. If only you would do this you would find me a ready partner with my heart, soul, and body.

Is this you? If it is, the God of heaven needs only your consent and cooperation to leave your past behind. His wisdom awaits your attention. Jesus is by your side, offering His sustaining grace that you may go forward. This letter is not only an appeal but also a prescription for the majority of us who are husbands.

Yet another woman shared, "The thing men don't seem to understand is that all the conventional wisdom regarding what women want is wrong. Oh, we're all attracted to the same basic things physically, but what really makes a man irresistible is strong moral character and unshakable self-control. With such a man we can let ourselves go, relax and not worry about his reactions. More than any other factor, *volatile emotions kill intimacy on every level.*"

VENDING MACHINE?

Are we hearing what our women are saying? The solution is simple. The question simply is, Will we follow it?

Women are different than we are, and yet somehow, after being attracted to them by those differences, we marry them and then expect them to be exactly like us, and it doesn't work. We become insensitive and display poor attitudes and then wonder why intimacy is lacking.

Christ encouraged us to love our wives as He loved the church, and He loved the church to death. He gave and gave of Himself until there was nothing left to give, and unless you love your wife this way, you are not fulfilling your role as a biblical husband.

Some husbands pick up the idea that their wives respond to warmth and affection and so they give that in order to get what they really want. But our wives are not vending machines to deposit our coins of nice words or kind deeds into once in a while to get our "candy bar." A wife always knows when she is being used—when you are just feeding in quarters expecting her to vend. She also knows when a Christlike husband is cherishing her. Any motivation short of coming under God and truly living for your wife is cheap and short-circuits all that could be and all that should be between you.

MAKE LOVE ALL DAY!

I met another woman whom I'll call Laura. Her husband, Brian, wanted me to straighten her out about her duty to fulfill his physical desires. I knew right away with a request like this that the problem was probably not Laura. Nevertheless, I agreed to meet with them, hoping I could help them find the keys to turning things around.

I found Laura similar to many women I have met in similar situations. She was upfront and honest and pretty much convinced things would never change.

"Mr. Hohnberger, after many years of frustration, I've concluded that I can choose to be 'happy' in my loveless marriage for the sake of my children. My husband wants me to be interested sexually, but I never get anything out of it. Often it only lasts a couple of minutes and after he gets his—he's done. He has no interest in pleasing me. I've given up the idea of getting anything out of the act."

Later when talking to Brian alone, I explained that lovemaking is not something that happens at night, but something that happens all day long and culminates at night, but I could see he was unimpressed. I encouraged him to spend time with Laura, at least an hour, to talk, to be affectionate, and make it enjoyable for her.

"If I've got to go through all that, I might as well go down to the corner," he retorted.

"With that attitude," I responded, "the corner is the only place you will be welcome, or at least your money will."

While I may find it hard to contemplate such callousness, unfortunately some women have to deal with it all the time. I met one quite fit, attractive woman who confessed that her husband insists she turn off the lights when she undresses because she doesn't look as good as she did when he married her. Yet another older woman told me that the kiss she got her wedding day was the only one of her married life, and she had had four children!

Men, what are we thinking? How can we behave this way? I'm not talking about improving your technique in lovemaking—although there is a place for that—I'm talking about improving your love! True love cares about the other person more than themselves. True love doesn't devalue people. I told the man who asked her to turn off the lights that he was lucky she did it with him at all. I wouldn't sleep in the same room with someone so cruel. Beauty and attraction are far more than skin-deep qualities—they come from inside a person and from the joining of two hearts.

CAN IT WORK?

The only thing that made Brian and Laura's situation hopeless was unwillingness. It didn't have to be that way. Often the mail brings us the sad news of ongoing failure for some of the couples we've counseled, but other times . . . well, read on and see what I mean.

> Dear Jim,
>
> Remember me? After so many years of hard times, I don't know how to tell you what has become of our marriage, so I guess I'll just have to share the word I find myself using more and more—bliss!
>
> You cannot believe the changes that happened in our life. My husband sold his business, Jim—HE SOLD IT! I never thought I'd live to see the day when he didn't run a business and just took time off, but he did it and he did it to find a walk with God and to spend time with me. I felt like a widow whose husband has miraculously come back to life. It had been so long, I

must confess I was suspicious at first and wondered what he was hiding from me. I thought he might be terminally ill and didn't want to tell me, but he was, for the first time since we were first married, interested in little ol' me. Today, my husband lives to spend time with me just like he did when we were dating. I am so happy. I wish every woman had a man like him.

We've had our struggles and it isn't always easy. For example, I've never had as much libido as he has and, as far as intimacy is concerned, I can take it or leave it. The way he used to be, I'd just as soon leave it. But he has really changed. He no longer pressures me or makes me feel guilty for not satisfying him. Instead, he genuinely cares for me—for me as a person! At first, I tested it for awhile. I wanted to see if his focus had really changed or if he was just manipulating me. I could hardly believe it! He truly and sincerely is no longer focused on getting what he wants. And, Jim, the amazing thing is that because he is so thoughtful, so kind, so considerate of me, I find myself actually wanting to be very sensitive to his physical needs because they are different than mine. We may never mesh perfectly, but we are moving towards each other rather than apart and that's what makes my heart sing.

But the best, the absolutely very best thing is that he is changing on the inside. He'd probably be embarrassed to know I told you this, but he is a very different man these days. In Christ, he has been working on his character weaknesses and while he is not perfect, I am thrilled with the changes. I desire more than anything else for him to draw even closer to Christ and continue to grow and overcome. I admire him so much. He is trying and in the strength of God succeeding more than I ever thought possible.

You know, Jim, as I see all the effort he is putting forth for me and the way he's changing on the inside, I find it nearly impossible to resist God's voice to my own heart. Our difficult days of struggle have given way to a rebirth of love and tenderness. God is good. As I said before, it's pure bliss.

In love again,

Sherry

This can be your wife's letter if you come under God's guidance to meet your spouse's real needs. True godly, self-denying love is the root of all lovemaking. When we seek only physical fulfillment in our relationship we will generally fail, but when we seek to selflessly love, physical intimacy almost always comes bubbling up to the surface as the byproduct. If you enter into this experience, you are about to enjoy a foretaste of heaven, not because of the byproducts, but because you will once more be in love with that wonderful woman you married. She was wonderful when you married her. She can be again.

Chapter 8
Intimacy: The Byproduct
Questions to Consider for Personal Inventory or Group Discussion

1. Do I love my wife for me? Or do I love her for her?
2. Do I love my wife like a little boy loves his ice-cream cone, or do I love her the way Christ loves His people?
3. Do I take my wife for granted all day and then expect her to be enthusiastic about lovemaking at night?
4. Do I spend more time in my newspapers, magazines, the Internet, e-mail, or radio than I do with my wife? Do I consistently allow time in our day for open-hearted communication?
5. Do I—on a regular basis—honestly pursue my wife as my queen?
6. Do I open the door for her, help her on with her coat, call her on the phone, or bring her unexpected flowers, cards, or gifts? Do I hug her, tell her she's pretty, compliment her cooking, do things on her "honey do" list?
7. Am I patient when she makes mistakes or does things differently than I would?
8. Does she know I do these things because I love her—not to get my "candy bar"?
9. Would my wife say I'm "in love" with her or that I love her?
10. Will I again make her the most pursued thing in my life?
11. Will I honestly take steps to change where change is needed?

"I'm Here for You— Period!"

Lo, I am with you alway, even unto the end of the world.
—Matthew 28:20

No different sound or unusual ring betrayed the urgency of the caller. It could have been just another call, but it wasn't. It was my son Matthew! At nine o'clock in the morning on October 7, 2004, I had no idea he had been trying to get ahold of me for more than an hour. We have come to associate wilderness living with unreliable phone service. It is an annoyance we have learned to live with, not to like. This morning, in particular, it was adding stress to our youngest son Andrew's day—a day that already promised to be stressful enough!

"Father, Andrew and Sarah are headed for the hospital. Her water broke! Can you come?"

"Tell Andrew we're on our way and our prayers are with them!"

We made a mad scramble as we grabbed those essential items like wallets, jackets, and cameras. In a flash we headed down the fifty miles of wilderness gravel road that lay between us and the ones we loved, the ones we were committed to, the ones I'd made a lifelong promise to. You see, the essence of fatherhood is a commitment to our children that says, "I am here for you—period! It doesn't make any difference how old you are, whether you are living in a way I agree with or not; in good times and in bad, I am here for you! From the time you are born until the time I die, I am going to be here for you." This commitment to be there for my children is what so moved me, as Sally and I drove those seemingly endless miles toward the birth of our first grandson.

Being there for my children meant I made sure I was there when they pounded in their first nail, chopped down their first tree, and baked that first loaf of bread. It was staying up late when they came home from that first date and being there when they came home from that first day on the job. I had been there for all these events and a thousand more with Andrew. For this big event, we had canceled all of our appointments for two weeks before and two weeks after Sarah's due date—just to be there to share their joy and support them through any difficulties.

Arriving at last, we were ushered into the hospital room, just ten minutes after the birth of little Landon James. He rested in his crib, quiet yet alert. But it was not the first sight of my new grandson that so captivated me. It was Andrew! Andrew was bending over his new little son, his hands grasping the tiny infant's, his gaze transfixed by Landon's. A sacred hush enveloped the room. The intensity of the connection being made between that little baby and his father was palpable. When at last he looked up at me, I thought I saw in his eyes the new weight of responsibility, the burden of the unknown, tempered with the joy of culminated love—a celebration of, perhaps, the greatest gift God has given the human family—the ability to reproduce in our own image.

As our eyes met, I couldn't hold back the tears even though I tried. His look communicated what words could not. To me it said, "Lord, help me to be to Landon James what You have been to me."

Unconditional commitment

I couldn't help remembering when I first became a father. I didn't understand true fatherhood. I didn't grasp the commitment needed to get the results desired. I was fully prepared to provide a comfortable home, food and clothing, a superior education, and a good social life. I thought that was about all there was to fatherhood.

It wasn't until I moved to the wilderness and invested real time with God that I came to understand in a new and fundamentally different way what fatherhood was all about. I discovered what it meant to be a father as I learned what it was like to have a heavenly Father—the kind the Bible refers to as Abba Father[1]—a daddy, a papa, one upon whom you can lean for support and find Him there for you.

Only as I came to know God for myself in my middle years did I grasp the idea that "God is here for me." He is here for me whether I am cooperating with Him or resisting Him. He loves me the same no matter what I am doing. He is my Abba Father, my Papa God. He not only loves me but also demonstrates that love with His coaching, His guidance, and His counseling. He is never intrusive, and yet He never abandons me, is ever by my side, and is incredibly long-suffering with my failures, my misunderstandings, my stupidity, and my outright rebellion. He promises, "I will never leave thee, nor forsake thee. So that we may boldly say, The Lord is my helper."[2] This is God's commitment to me, and God's commitment to you! It took me years to finally get it, but I am coming to understand my Father God.

Standing in that hospital room, tears falling unashamedly down my cheeks, I could see Andrew had come to the same understanding and at a much younger age than I did. Anyone could have seen his commitment as he stood by his son's side in those first minutes of life. He was going to be there for Landon James—period! That's a real father!

Being a father is so simple and yet so very profound that it escapes most of us, perhaps because of its very simplicity. We tend to think that anything worthwhile has to be difficult and complicated. I won't downplay the fact that true fatherhood requires much difficult self-denial, but it is not complicated. In fact, there are really only two types of characteristics or two sides of being an *abba* father, like our heavenly *Abba* Father.

TWO SIDES OF LOVE

There is the tender side of fatherhood consisting of what I refer to as the softer virtues. These encompass such things as gentleness, meekness, kindliness, love, and mercy. They are expressed in the home by denying oneself for the good of others. Abba fathers live to bring others joy even though it costs them of their time and their own desires, recreation, or

1. See Galatians 4:6.
2. Hebrews 13:5, 6.

interests. Having tasted of their heavenly Father's love, they fill the home's atmosphere with joy that springs from within. The tender side of an abba father gives a soft answer when he feels provoked, because he has learned to filter his words and actions through his own Abba Father. An abba father patiently endures all things, knowing that God is in control of even the most unpleasant of life's circumstances.

But the abba father is not just soft and tender; he possesses the firmer virtues as well. These include courage, strength, energy, perseverance, integrity, and justice. He will not wait until every obstacle is removed before he acts. He doesn't follow the crowd. Instead, he leads others to follow God. He stands firmly, as it were, in God's shadow, possessing the perseverance of a hero to resist evil and promote good.

Both the tender virtues and the firmer virtues are essential. Without our Abba Father, however, we are destined to be imbalanced. You see, a man who has only the softer virtues is not balanced any more than is a man who has only the firmer virtues. Either imbalance can pervert these traits to the point where they are no longer virtues, but vices.

Think of the lessons of history. Neville Chamberlain was a man whose character was rich in the softer virtues, while Adolf Hitler had only the hard, firm virtues. Chamberlain thought he could gain peace at almost any cost and has gone down in history a pitiful example of the follies of appeasement. Hitler walked out of their meetings thinking he had gained everything. Drunk with power and success, he felt he could conquer the world and so planted the seeds of his own destruction. So it is with every man who thinks he can exercise these virtues apart from their Author and the balance He alone imparts. Disconnected from God, both the firm and soft virtues will ultimately leave us all unbalanced. But when cultivated under the influence of God's Spirit, both sides provide essential tools that enable us to *be there for our children—period!*

We all have a tendency to be imbalanced on one side or the other. Only in Christ can we find balance and cultivate these virtues for truly unselfish purposes. I have a strong natural tendency to lean toward the firmer side, and God has had to work extensively with me, developing a balance with tenderness, and one key text he used to teach me is Ephesians 6:4.

NUMERO UNO

Most men I talk to have heard or read the words of Ephesians 6:4, "Fathers, provoke not your children to wrath; but bring them up in the nurture and admonition of the Lord." However, few of us seem to have thought out exactly what this means; I know I hadn't when I first became a father. But as I began pondering this text with my heavenly Father, I began to wonder what He could possibly do that would really provoke me to wrath. Do you know what I came up with? If God had no time for me, that would really provoke me. This would make me want to turn my back on Him and go to the world, my friends, and a myriad less-than-uplifting activities, all of which would welcome me and have time for me.

But how often do we do that to *our* children? How often do they feel that other things rob them of our time? When I saw this, I began to alter my priorities. I wanted my children to understand that they were more important than my career, my hobbies, my friends, my sports, my newscasts, my Internet, and my newspaper. I wanted them to find in me an abba father who nurtured at the right time and was there to admonish them in the Lord when needed. To help accomplish this, I set aside every evening after six-thirty as family time. Pretty soon, it was our favorite time of day. It was time Sally and I devoted exclusively to our boys. It gave us time to play, work, teach, train, and talk with them more than any other period of their day.

When we played with them, there were things that crossed their wills and we had to help them through some hard choices. When we worked together it would often reveal character weakness that needed to be addressed, and once more we had opportunity to work with them on the real lifework—character development. When we talked, we had the precious opportunity to see deep into their souls as they pulled back the curtain to share what was on their hearts.

I learned these priceless lessons through hard experience and many missteps. I found I had to counsel my children, not scold them. I realized that, young as my boys were, they were free moral agents—meaning they had the ability to choose between right and wrong. Enlisting their will for right rather than forcing them with my superior willpower paid large dividends in time. If I could enlist their power of choice to carry out God's will for them, then He could empower them just the same as He does me when I choose to obey Him. It was here I adopted the position of being their coach rather than their commander. It worked so much better!

The Lord made it clear to me that I was to be their instructor and teacher; but I was not their *lord*. I started to get excited! These principles were exactly the same ones God used with me and uses with all of us. He says, "Come now, and let us reason together."[3] The God of the universe adopts the attitude of "Come on, we are in this together; let's work it out." If He could do this for me, surely I could do the same for my own children, and that's what I sought to do.

Cheated, yet enriched

I will never forget the day Andrew arrived home devastated. He had met this nice Christian family in his business. They were of the same faith, had the same belief system, and the same mind-set—or so Andrew thought. They had come to him hoping he would help them find that just-right country property—the one that could become their special place. Andrew printed out packages of prospective properties; the clients would look them over and drive by any that interested them. Andrew would then arrange a showing if they wanted to see more. He put forth a lot of effort and showed them a number of properties, but they had yet to find that one property that caught their eye.

One day they drove by one that seemed to have real possibilities. They were captivated, and the owners, who happened to be out in the yard, invited them in and gave them a tour of the property. They loved it! Andrew would have been so happy that one of the places he recommended for them was working out, but he didn't know. They never told him. The owners talked this Christian family—Andrew's clients—into working directly with *their* listing agent so that they could save a couple of percent on the commission. The couple purchased the property, and Andrew never knew what had happened until he made a routine follow-up call. He was devastated, his trust in humanity momentarily shattered. He had a lot of issues to deal with—the hurt, the rejection, the misuse and, in fact, the stealing of his time and talents. When Andrew came home that night, he needed to talk.

---

3. Isaiah 1:18.

So talk we did. We talked about what had happened. We considered that often in life we have to deal with ingratitude and indifference. We thought about the life of Christ. Rarely were those He helped or healed even grateful. Andrew and I reviewed the story of the ten lepers, in which only one returned to thank Jesus. Andrew considered his options. He had been raised to live by godly principles, doing right because it is right, and treating others the way Christ treats us. He knew no good could come from harboring feelings of hurt and bitterness. At length, he decided to take the high road and surrender his feelings to Jesus. In so doing, he found peace and victory over his emotions.

Months later, the family who had so misused his time apologized and sent him a token check for his gas. Nevertheless, what mattered in that situation was not the other family but that his family—his father— was there for him with a heart that could feel his anguish. That's the tender side of fatherhood.

CHARACTER OVER COMFORT

However, there is the other side to being there for them—the side that challenges! God possesses a challenging side. He nurtures, encourages, and helps, but He also calls us to do hard things, to make difficult decisions, to suffer discomfort and inconvenience, all divinely designed to nudge us to grow. He is there for our comfort, but He is concerned with far more than our comfort—He cares about our character. I needed to learn from God how to use the firmer virtues I already possessed and use them to challenge my sons as God had challenged me in my life, to move out of their comfort zones and do new things. This was a totally new experience for me as well. I had thought my firmness a virtue for commanding my sons, but under God's tutoring the firmness was to be the encouraging nudge to strengthen and direct the construction of their characters.

When Matthew and Andrew were about eight and ten years old, they were intrigued with horseback riding. "Father, couldn't we have horses?"

"Boys, that would be fun, wouldn't it?"

"Yes, Father, yes! Can we get some?"

"Boys, why don't you go down and visit Mrs. Schmidt? She has horses. Why don't you see if you can work out a deal with her? An older woman like her surely needs the help of strong young men like you, and perhaps she could pay you for your labor with some time riding her horses."

I didn't share all my thoughts with my sons, but I was concerned. Space to keep horses and places to ride in the wilderness were not a problem, but I didn't want to spend time and money buying the beautiful animals, installing fences and stables, buying oats and hay, as well as paying for veterinarian bills, only to have the boys lose interest in just a short time. So I had come up with an alternative and in so doing, had selected one that would really challenge them.

Andrew and Matthew looked at each other, and I knew what they were thinking. Mrs. Schmidt was an elderly widow who was so stern and gruff that she intimidated even me, and no one intimidates me! I wondered if the boys' desire to ride horses would outweigh their reluctance to approach this crusty old horsewoman.

Their longings overcame their dread, and soon I saw two little fellows in jeans and suspenders bicycling down the dusty road to Mrs. Schmidt's place. They were gone for nearly three hours, and I wondered what was going on, but I soon found out. Matthew and Andrew came back, more infuriated and humiliated than I'd ever seen them.

"Father, it's not fair!" blurted out Matthew. "We worked out a deal with Mrs. Schmidt to weed her garden for one hour, and she was going to pay us each one hour of horseback riding."

"So we weeded her garden for a full hour—" began Andrew.

"And we did a good job, too!" asserted Matthew. "She let me ride for a half hour, and then Andrew got on for a half hour."

Andrew continued, "Matthew was getting ready to ride his last half hour when she suddenly yells out, 'Time's up! You've had your ride. Now head for home.' I tried to reason with her, Father. It was very clear that we were supposed to each get one full hour of riding for one full hour of working. But she wouldn't give in. She just went on and on about how much horses cost and how much saddles cost and how much feed costs and on and on. She's just a mean old grump, and someone should put her in her place. Won't you go down and talk to her, Father? Please?"

Both boys looked at me, their eyes pleading for justice, and they were sure Father was their man for the hour!

DON'T FALTER—FACE IT!

After sending up a petition for wisdom to Abba, my Father, I said, "Boys, it's time for you two to become men. You must learn to stand on your own and face the Mrs. Schmidts of the world. You need to go back to her and politely approach her again with your bargain."

Oh, how those two boys struggled. To face that domineering, feisty old crank again seemed far too much to ask. I pressed them, prayed with them, and encouraged them until they finally pedaled down the road again toward the scene of their conflict.

They were home again very quickly with their tails between their legs. They had gone to the back door and knocked timidly. Mrs. Schmidt was surprised to see them back so soon and was wild with anger. She dragged them into her dining room, sat them down and poured forth the same litany of horse owner's expenses and who did they think they were and no way were they going to ride anymore. Matthew and Andrew tried their best diplomacy to calm her down and reason with her, but she would have none of it. She soon shooed them out the back door, letting the screen door close with a final bang.

"Father, she is impossible. You can't reason with her. Maybe you could, but we can't. Father, you must go talk to her yourself. We can't."

"I am sorry this is hard, but you must learn how to handle the Mrs. Schmidts of the world."

"Aren't you going to come with us, Father?"

"No." Their faces fell in discouragement. "But I *am* going to tell you exactly what to do, and it will work! Will you do it?"

Two sets of eyes dubiously studied mine and then slowly nodded agreement.

"Mrs. Schmidt has a big heart hidden down deep under her cranky demeanor. She has been hurt deeply sometime in the past, and so she hurts other people so they cannot hurt her. Here is what you do."

"Go back to her house and knock on her door. She'll be angry and likely chew you out again. You just keep your mouths shut until she runs out of things to fuss about. Then say to her, 'Mrs. Schmidt, can we give you a hug and a kiss?'"

My boys weren't real sure of this plan, but they trusted me enough to give it a try.

The scenario went just as I predicted. Mrs. Schmidt opened the door for the third time and just exploded. "What do you boys want now? What part of 'no' don't you understand?" And off she went on another tirade.

The boys waited patiently until she ran out of steam and then looked up at her with eyes of innocence and simply asked, "Mrs. Schmidt, can we hug you and kiss you?"

There was a moment of silence and then all the barriers came down. Mrs. Schmidt opened her door and invited them in. Amidst their hugs and kisses, her cold selfishness melted away.

My boys got their fair share of horseback riding and gained a new friend. Mrs. Schmidt depended on Matthew and Andrew after that day to help her with odd jobs until she sold her place and moved away. More than that, though, my boys learned to face intimidating odds, face a losing situation, and not be overcome by the evil, but to overcome the evil with good. I've never been prouder of them.

This was using firmness to be there for my boys—period! I was there to urge them to face a difficult situation rather than to avoid it. The softer virtues of sympathy exercised exclusively in this situation would have actually hindered my boys' development. Firmness exercised by their father helped them to develop firmness within their own souls.

Dependable

As my boys grew older, I continued to learn from my heavenly Father how to be an abba father for them. They learned to respect my tender side and to value my firm side because they knew that the heart beneath both sides beat with unselfish love for them.

When Andrew was twenty-two and living on his own and getting ready to marry, I got this letter from him:

My Dear Father,

You have always been and continue to be as strong as a rock for principles and a place I can always go to when I need to be encouraged onward and upward.

When things get rough in the business world, I can always come home and *know* my father will be there to talk to.

Many times I don't even have to talk to you, because just your presence alone speaks wisdom to me. I know I'm not much of a talker, but I learn 90 percent of what I need just by watching you.

You are and have always been the quintessential father.

Love,

Andrew

In just a few words, Andrew shared a blessed view of his abba father—both the firm and the tender side. I share this to encourage you, not to build myself up, for I know better than anyone that only the wondrous grace of God has provided my son with this view of his father in spite of my human failings.

"You have always been and continue to be strong as a rock for principle." The problem far too many young people face in nice Christian homes is that they see both belief and actions, but never the twain shall meet. Their fathers are firm and demanding for the sake of their own selfish interests, but when principle crosses their inclination, they waver. The strength of Jesus was that He did not merely espouse principles; He lived them every day.

PRINCIPLE VS. PRIDE

One of the principles I strove to live before my boys was Christ's command, "Husbands, love your wives, even as Christ also loved the church, and gave himself for it."[4] This has not come naturally for me, and my boys have watched the heavenly Father work with their father. They have seen me wrestle with my own strong inclinations toward evil and find grace to follow principle rather than my own desires.

I remember blowing up at Sally once—right in front of Matthew and Andrew—because she had spent more money on some blue jeans than I thought she should have. I knew she could have gotten the jeans cheaper somewhere else, and I wouldn't even listen to her reasons for not doing it my way. I was sure I was right. The Lord spoke to me the following morning and told me otherwise. I was willing to apologize to Sally, but then the

---

4. Ephesians 5:25.

Lord reminded me that little eyes and ears had seen and heard and that I needed to admit my wrong in their presence. You know, that was a lot harder! I didn't like humbling myself in front of my sons, but God knew the boys needed to see their father yielding to principle rather than pride.

ALWAYS THERE

Remember Andrew had written, "a place I can always go to when I need to be encouraged onward and upward." Not long ago, friends talked us into skiing in Sun Valley, Idaho. In our type of ministry we travel so much that I was resistant at first to the idea of taking time off to travel again, but I finally agreed, and now we were on the slopes for one of the most glorious skiing days I have ever seen. The freshly fallen snow was groomed to perfection. The sun's balmy glow matched the warmth of the friendship that surrounded me, and I was just beginning to soak in the relaxation and joy . . . and then my cell phone rang. I am not a cell phone junkie. I had only brought it on the mountain so our group of friends could keep in touch with each other. However, it was Andrew, and he needed to talk to his father!

The snow is perfect, my friends are waiting, but I couldn't say no. I had promised Andrew that I would be there for him. Vacation or no vacation, convenient or inconvenient, Andrew is more important than any of my personal interests. I told everyone to go ahead without me. I would catch up later.

He just wanted to talk out a problem. He didn't need me to tell him the solution; he just needed a sounding board, and it was my duty—no, it was my joyous privilege—to be there for him. Andrew left our conversation ready to face his difficulty with courage and love. I skied after my friends, feeling energized by my son's confidence.

RELIABLE AND FUN

My two sons have very different personalities and preferences, and yet they both need the same commitment from their father. Matthew was twenty-three when he wrote, "I don't know where I would be without your counsel and insight, which I treasure and highly appreciate. You are reliable as the mountains and as fun as the river. As the years have gone by you have taught me the importance of many things, but the most important is Christ being the center focus of my life."

Here once more is outlined the two sides to *abba,* father—the tender side and the principled side. I loved to see him write that I'm as reliable as the mountains because he has only distant memories of living in the flat lands. The mighty Rocky Mountains have been his constant companions. They were always there. I hope any memories are gone forever of the days before I knew better, the days when I was not always there for my children.

The second metaphor might not sound like a compliment to some— especially if they are accustomed to the smelly, polluted bodies of water common in urban areas. But you have to know our river! The North Fork of the Flathead River runs just a short walk away from our home. It's a lovely swirling mass of glacier melt tumbling over a myriad of stones amid the grandeur and rugged beauty of this last wilderness valley. From the boys' earliest years, the river has been an endless source of recreation both on and off the water, and Matthew absolutely loves to canoe and kayak. Guess who taught him, and guess who still loves to play with him? Yes, in my son's eyes I'm as fun as the river! Are you the same to your children?

REFLECTING CHRIST

But there is something deeper to fatherhood than just standing for principles and being fun. There is the task of conveying that making Christ first, last, and best gives our lives meaning and purpose, while fulfilling the deepest longings and desires of the human heart. This is indeed the work of a lifetime. Sometimes you aren't sure how much of what you've tried to pass on to your children has become incorporated in their own souls. I got a chance to find out when Matthew was in his early twenties.

"Father, I was so embarrassed for one of my clients today," he blurted one day after work.

"What happened?" I asked, my curiosity rising.

"Well, I took them up to Whale Creek to look at that get-a-way cabin I have listed, and when I opened the door there was a picture of a naked woman staring at me from the wall behind the couch."

"What did you do?"

"Well, I didn't know what to do, so I quickly shut the door."

"What then?" I inquired, captivated with the idea of him suddenly shutting the door with his clients standing right there behind him.

"I asked them to wait for a moment by the car. Then I went back in . . . but I didn't look up, Father. I simply reached up and took the picture down and shoved it under the couch. Then I brought the clients back in."

"What did you tell them? They must have wondered what happened."

"I explained that it wouldn't have been proper for me to show them the house until I fixed something."

"I'm proud of you, son. You stood for principle, and I don't need to tell you that you did the right thing."

Biblical purity in a young man is so rare these days that it seems odd, but Matthew, up to that point, had never seen a sensual portrayal of the female form, and I took the conversation further. "What did *you* think of the picture, Matthew?

"Father, it was disgusting to see her so degraded. Why do people do that to women?"

That's a good question, isn't it? I knew at that point the woman Matthew married would never have to worry about being devalued or being viewed as merely a sex object. Matthew's value system attached such respect to women that he could not bear to see even an anonymous woman exposed in a picture. Very few young men at his age would have done the same, and we are all the poorer for the loss of such virtues.

The key to his behavior, I believe, was summed up in his note to me. "As the years have gone by you have taught me the importance of many things, but the most important is Christ being the center focus of my life."

Matthew had come to this position after years of example, and it is a sobering lesson for all of us. What did your children see in you last night, or last week, or this past year? Do they see continual compromise in entertainment, language, recreation, or ethics? What principles are you teaching in your treatment of their mother? Do they see someone who is as reliable as the mountains, someone who is making Christ the center focus of his life in his business, marriage, and home?

If not, it is not too late to recapture the two sides of abba father and redeem the time we wasted in skewed priorities. If you do pick up this work, you will be a true son of Abba Father and a hero to your children and to your wife. That is what my son taught me.

You have led the way
You've outlined the path
You've shown us the goal
You've surpassed them all.
Because God is your guide
You are my hero.
—Matthew Hohnberger, 1999

CHAPTER 9

"I'm Here for You—Period!"

Questions to Consider for Personal Inventory or Group Discussion

1. What would my children honestly say that I live for? Do they know there is nothing more important in the world to me than them?
2. Does my presence in my home bring joy?
3. Am I imbalanced more toward the softer virtues or the firmer virtues?
4. Do I give my children more undivided attention than I give my hobbies, my news, my sports, or my religious work? Do I spend quality and quantity time with my children consistently?
5. Do they know they can count on me to listen and help when they face disappointment? Am I a coach to my children as God is a coach to me?
6. Can my children really tell me what is on their hearts without fear of being scolded, ridiculed, or ignored?
7. Do I tell them that I am proud of them? That I believe in them? That I love them?
8. Do I challenge them to face difficult things? Am I there to encourage and instruct them as they face those hard things?
9. Do my children respect me because my belief and my actions match? Would they say I am their hero?
10. Do they see me treating their mother with respect and tenderness?

Building Men

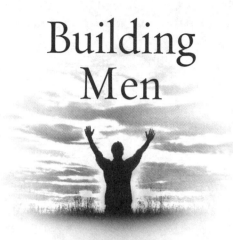

Where is the flock that was given thee, thy beautiful flock?
—*Jeremiah 13:20*

I had just returned home from my youngest son Andrew's wedding with all the excitement, the joys, and the memories. Matthew, my oldest, had married less than three months before, and two weddings in that short a time frame can take a lot out of a father. I spent the day just getting caught up until six-thirty in the evening. This had been my favorite time of day—what we called Family Time, the time I always set aside to draw my family together to play, to talk, to read books together, to work on some special project, and most of all to demonstrate in a meaningful way how special each family member was to us. I never allowed business or even my ministry to intrude upon this time. I set it aside exclusively for quality interaction with my boys.

But that evening it was quiet, far too quiet. I found myself leaning in the doorway of my boys' bedroom gazing at two empty beds. So much had happened in that house. It's hard to imagine how important this little log home has become not only to our family but to so many who've been touched by our message all around the world. I stood there reflecting on the culmination of one era and the start of another.

I sat down on one bed as I considered the ceremonies that had launched the boys into the establishment of their own homes with two of the sweetest girls divine Providence could provide. I smiled at the memory because each wedding was unique, and God had honored each wedding in a very special way. In addition, I'd had the joyous privilege of officiating at both ceremonies. There was a lump in my throat just reviewing the memories, but it's hard to be sad for long when you know your children are fulfilling their God-given destiny.

PRIVATE JOKE?

Matthew was twenty-five years old, Andrew twenty-three. They possessed strong characters enabling them to stand for what they believe is right regardless of the odds that face them. They don't automatically follow the crowd, whether they are at home, at their businesses, in church, or with nonbelievers. They are sensitive to remaining under the control of God.

I'd seen them tested again and again in touchy situations. For example, they consistently refused to play the businessmen's games of loose talk and office politics and often missed the meaning of jokes because slang words and double meanings are not a part of their vocabulary. In fact, one man who worked with Matthew told me, "Jim, there was this situation of which I am not proud, but I feel compelled to tell you about. I got mad at your son one day, and I cussed him out to his face for quite a while. I never saw anyone so calm in the face of that type of language."

I smiled, more to myself than to the man, but it irked him to no end. "Are you laughing at me?" he demanded. "Is this some #!*! private joke between Matthew and you?" He was really insecure, as are most people who feel the need to somehow buttress the force of their words with the use of curses.

"No," I assured him, "I am not laughing at you, just at the situation. My son is self-controlled, but that is not why he responded to you the way he did. It is funny because he has never heard such talk in all his life and, frankly, he probably had no clue what you were saying."

He looked at me with a look of complete incredulity on his face and then as the full meaning of my words sank in, he burst out laughing—this time at himself. At last, when he could speak again, he turned to me with a seriousness I could not mistake and said, "You've done well, Jim, by protecting him. He's a good kid. I wish I didn't know half the junk I've learned."

However, testing doesn't always take the form of conflict. Indeed, often it comes in the guise of friendship. The problem is that when you stand for something, people want to see if it is really what you stand for or just the same talk they hear from others. Matthew and Andrew, being raised in the wilderness with godly values and self-control as an inherent part of their characters, proved a curiosity to many of their co-workers. Young men freely choosing to embrace principle, independent of any parental domination, is such a rare thing in today's society, it is totally natural for people to want to test their convictions.

Devil's advocate

Raised in a simple home with simple wholesome food, their tastes have never been cultivated toward junk foods, and hence appetite holds little power over them, a fact their co-workers soon discovered by observation. One gentleman decided to see if this was really their conviction and played devil's advocate when Matthew was at the office for meetings. Virtually everyone was enjoying some luscious chocolate éclairs, but Matthew declined.

"Come on, it's OK," the man coaxed.

"No. Thank you anyway."

"Really, it's all right. Go ahead and have one. Your brother had one at the last meeting."

Matthew smiled, "Thank you for your hospitality. Perhaps I should explain. It is not a matter of what I can or can't do. After all, I'm a grown man. But it is a matter of my choices and their effect upon my life and health. I'm careful to guard my health, and such a rich treat might taste good, but would it help me to have a clear mind or a strong body? I also believe I know my brother far better than you think. Andrew would never eat food like this. Shall I call Andrew and ask him to come up here so you can explain exactly what you saw him eating?"

"Ah . . . no . . . that really won't be necessary . . . I . . . uh . . . might have been mistaken."

When your children are raised in the public eye like mine have been, people seem to feel the need to test them, and to do so they have frequently tried to play my boys against one another. They view it almost like a sport. But let me assure you that Satan doesn't and neither does

God. Satan loves to get people to play the old divide-and-conquer game, and he and his willing accomplices have used it with great success in the families of our day.

TINKERERS

Some of these people have tried to invite themselves into the boys' private affairs. Being in the ministry and talking about our personal experiences causes some people to feel that we may be mixed up on a point here and there. Certainly there is nothing wrong with this, for they are free to draw their own conclusions. However, I have often wished they could have dealt with their disagreements in a more mature and constructive manner. Unfortunately, some feel it is not only their right to straighten us out but also their religious duty.

Because of these attitudes, my boys have, from the time they were quite young, had to resist some very strong efforts of certain adults to get them to do things their way. Typically, these people have over-dominated their own children, and they want mine to submit to them in the same manner.

When my boys respectfully asked for evidence from Scripture to back these assertions and demands, these individuals had been unable to back up their assertions, and I have been greeted with complaints about how "unsubmissive" my son or sons are. But are my sons really nonsubmissive or have they just been taught to think for themselves? I believe it is the latter. Furthermore, I do not believe we do our children any favors when we do not train them to think and act for themselves. As parents, we desire to lead children into the pathway to heaven, and I believe that is what many of these people who have tried to influence our children sincerely think they are doing. I also believe when our young people ask us for our reasons we should be able to provide them an answer based on the Word of God and common sense. Will Christianity be safely delivered to the next generation's hands if we have not taught our young people how to reason and discern truth for themselves? I have met so many who take a short-sighted goal of having their children appear like perfect little soldiers following along in line, looking great to their parents and everyone else—everyone else, that is, except God.

Yes, we raised two strong men who stand out from the world, from our decaying society and our troubled church. They are as true to duty as the needle to the pole. They will not be bought or sold. They have become what we raised them to be. My eyes lovingly caressed the photos of the boys on the opposite wall, while my memory saw two cute, cuddly boys ages four and six sleeping in these two beds, blissfully unaware of my struggles as a father and my commitment to make them a priority.

You see, when we moved to the wilderness of Montana, I had a sense that I wanted to raise my boys to be real men, not just clones of society or mimics of watered-down Christianity, but I had no practical idea how to do it. I hadn't the slightest idea of *how* to be a godly father!

TIME

I knew how to provide financially for them. I was a successful businessman. They would never lack for proper food, clothing, shelter, or education. But the realization kept nagging me that other fathers, both in the world and in the church, did that and still ended up with children ill-prepared for life. What was missing? How could I fill the gap so that my boys could be men who would stand when all others bow?

Sitting in their room that evening, God replayed with me a video of all their growing-up years. What worked for me is what I will share with you. God did not see fit to give Sally and me girls, so I'm going to talk about building men. But the same principles apply to developing virtuous women.

The bottom-line principle God taught me is very simple, yet it is profound in its implications and results. It says, "Every day, I'm here for *you!* I don't have all the answers. I don't have your future all laid out. But every day I'll go to God. He and I will step you through whatever you may face." It means becoming like a wheat plant—giving my whole life to bring the next generation to full maturity. It can be synthesized in one four-letter word: *time*. Time for you! Time to play, time to work, time to talk, time to nurture and admonish, and time to worship and pray. I didn't know it at the time, but I was setting out on a road that would win their hearts for life!

PLAYING TRUCKIE

Taking time to play with my boys did not come easily for me at first. I chuckled as I remembered those first few awkward playtimes. After all, I was a successful businessman. It felt a bit humiliating to play "truckie"! But that is where God started working with me. He said, *"Jim, lay aside your sense of importance and become as a little child."*

I took my two boys outside and, using some logs from the nearby forest, built a sandbox with them. Then we drove my old pick-up down to the river and dug sand out of a sand bank to fill it. Of course, after that, we spent hours building roads and tunnels and going *"vroom, vroom"* with our truckies. My boys thought it was great, and I came to know my sons in a way I never had before. They began to open their little hearts to me simply and naturally because I was there with them. I began to catch on to God's wisdom.

We played kickball, a variety of couch games, hide-and-seek, and tag. Sometimes, we just enjoyed a simple game of dominoes, marbles, or pick-up sticks. We never kept score—just played for innocent fun. We laughed and learned to enjoy one another.

As Matthew and Andrew grew older, our expeditions became more challenging. Hiking led to backpacking, mountain biking, caving, rappelling, skiing, kayaking, and mountain climbing. Our home is located just across the river from Glacier National Park, and our boys set the record on being the youngest climbers to make the ascent of a number of peaks.

Over the years our family had read Sam Campbell's books, and as Sam shared his experience finding the hidden lake in Canada's Quetico Provincial Park, which he called Sanctuary Lake, Matthew's imagination was kindled. Our sixteen-year-old Matthew was taken with the idea of finding Sanctuary Lake—so taken, he was almost obsessed with the idea. He couldn't think of any outing more wonderful than retracing Sam's steps to this lake that was hidden "somewhere east of sunset and somewhere west of dawn."

"But, Matthew," I protested when he asked me if we could go to Quetico. "We moved all the way from Wisconsin to live in this great mountainous wilderness, and we have not yet explored all its lakes or climbed all its mountains. Why should we drive all the way back to northern Minnesota and the Canadian canoe wilderness just to paddle our canoe? Why not do something close to home?"

But Matthew kept on dreaming and talking about his dreams. I went to God. *Lord, Matthew's idea is just not practical. It would be expensive and inconvenient. Can I squash it?*

God said, *"Invest yourself in Matthew's dreams. Don't make him live exclusively in your box. Enter into his aspirations."*

So we told Matthew that if he would do the research and planning needed for this expedition, we would go as a family to find Sanctuary Lake. Matthew did, and we did. We spent two weeks canoeing in the wilderness—just the four of us. We built all kinds of irreplaceable memories, and we did find Sanctuary Lake. And you know, I fell in love with that wilderness. It is still my favorite place to go for a vacation, for time away to "be still" and know God.

GEARS IN A WELL-OILED MACHINE

My sons liked their playtime with Father. It knit our hearts together. It communicated to them that I enjoyed them for who they are. Reflecting on those memories warmed my heart that October evening. But life is not all play. There is real work to be done, and I saw the need to educate my boys in such a way that when they would be men with homes of their own, they would know how to operate them like a well-oiled machine. We wanted our boys to become men who shoulder their responsibilities and bear them well—not look for the easy path. Sally and I taught them that they were very important "gears" in the machinery of our home and that when we all worked responsibly and cheerfully, work was never a burden.

Gazing around their room now, I saw several work projects the boys had completed alone and some that we had done together—like installing a sky light, adding in walls, doors, bookcases, and trim. More than the woodwork, I valued the character building each of those projects represented.

Many people who became acquainted with our family when our boys were older concluded they must have come from the womb helpful and cooperative, but the truth is nearly the opposite. Sitting on my son's bed, I can still hear Sally robotically asking six-year-old Matthew and four-year-old Andrew, "Did you brush your teeth? Have you made your bed? Did you comb your hair? Did you do . . . ?" I became very frustrated with this parental reminder service because it seemed incompatible with our goal of having them become self-governing. They had to be self-governing someday, and if someday, why not start right now?

We made up little charts showing their tasks such as brushing their teeth, making their beds, stacking the wood by the wood stove, doing dishes, and taking out the trash. We explained that these were to be done without reminders to the best of their ability, and, of course, we kept our expectations consistent with their age and abilities.

If these jobs were not done, there would be some consequence such as extra chores to exercise their weak work skills or perhaps the loss of some privilege. It took time and much more training than punishment for them to become proficient, and there were days when it seemed they would never learn. Still they grew in knowledge and responsibility, and so did we as they learned to master these basic skills of life. You may view these things as minor, but we have learned from observation that many a child enters adulthood without the habit of making their bed each day.

INCREASING RESPONSIBILITIES

As they got a little older we gave them more responsibilities. They learned to do the meal preparation and how to plan a grocery list and menu. They were educated in the subtleties of laundry and eventually in running the whole household for a day. They had to learn how to delegate and command, so if Andrew was in charge of making meals for the day, and he asked me to scrub the potatoes, I had to scrub the potatoes! They learned all the facets of gardening from preparing the ground to planting the seeds, cultivating the crops, and harvesting and canning the fruit.

Sally primarily supervised and trained them in the intricacies of domestic labor, but I recognized that for my boys to become men, they needed to master the more masculine duties as well. That was my primary responsibility—Sally was not cut out for this—so I began while they were very young by helping them to fix their truckies. As they got older, I recruited them for washing the car and assisting me in the maintenance of our vehicles. Did they get in my way? Of course they did. But I didn't let them know it. I told them their help was indispensable, and in time, with practice, that was true.

Diversity

They mastered carpentry. Beginning with some rather crude birdhouses, they progressed to building workbenches in my garage and wood decks and railings for the cabin. They gained experience working with concrete and rock by hauling river rock to our place and constructing a rock wall around the perimeter foundation of our home.

They mowed and raked the lawn. In the winter, they shoveled snow, operated the snow blower, and learned to clear the driveway using the plow. Of course, they learned to cut firewood. One of the most dangerous tasks of wilderness living is felling trees and cutting them up to burn. I taught my boys to become masters of the job.

Intro to the business world

As they progressed through their early teen years, I began training them for business. I took them with me when I did real estate work—interviews, showings, walking property lines, writing up offers, even closings and office work. I didn't know what type of work they would eventually embrace, but the same basic principles apply almost universally to every business—things like customer service, honesty, thoroughness, and hard work.

We allowed our sons to begin speaking for our ministry at seminars, and this taught them the basics of sermon preparation. It also forced them to become comfortable meeting strangers and talking to adults in an interesting manner. In a similar way, we pushed them to take control of their own education in home-schooling—something we did not only out of choice, but also out of necessity because of our location in the wilderness, where there were no schools. As part of their training in self-government we allowed them to work ahead and take days off if they wished.

The program of child rearing we engaged in is what a banker might call "front end loaded," meaning that the vast majority of the effort is at the very beginning and slowly decreases as time goes on. By the time our boys were in their teens, our early efforts began paying off. The boys worked well in the home and for other people. They began working for contractors, building homes in the valley. They contracted to paint and stain homes. Andrew started his own business selling bunk beds he built himself. He negotiated an arrangement to set up his display model in the local mall. This business exposure taught them how to meet strangers, do a presentation, close a deal, and make the sale. In addition they had to book appointments, make business decisions, manage their time, think things out using common sense, as well as learn bookkeeping, money management, and how to handle checking accounts.

I found out in my own career that true freedom in employment is having your own business, not in working for a corporation, even though many fine people do such work and are not bothered by it. I, however, loved being my own boss and having full control over my destiny. I raised my sons and designed their whole educational program to give them the skills needed to make a living running their own businesses. This didn't force them into choosing to run their own business, but it did make such a choice a viable option if they desired it.

Working together like a well-oiled machine! Playing together as the best of friends! Laughing and enjoying one another! We are a family! We are not scattered, distracted, living separate lives—our hearts are tightly knit. And all that time together in play and work naturally spawns talk time.

HEART TO HEART

I stood up and walked over to the window. Watching our deer peacefully grazing on our lawn stirred so many memories of evenings just like this one. My eyes misted at the thoughts of the four of us visiting on the porch or in the living room while our wild friends browsed.

We encouraged our boys to confide in us about anything and everything on their minds. In our home, everyone has a right to his own opinion. And everyone is allowed time to express themselves without interruption as long as they do it respectfully.

While they were little, the boys loved to chatter. When the two of them chopped down their first tree, they had to tell us the whole story embellished with every itty-bitty detail—arms waving in demonstration and eyes sparkling. When they sledded down the hill, they wanted to reenact the entire event. These were far more interesting stories to them than anything you could find on the six o'clock news. To Sally and me this was simply childish prattle, but we trained ourselves to be interested in their conversations. What would have happened to their hearts if I had tuned them out in order to hear the latest from the White House or Wall Street?

Young children ask a myriad of questions. We took the time to listen, explain, and expound. We encouraged them to express their thoughts and their ideas. We didn't cut them off. When the two boys got ticked off at each other, as siblings and all human beings do, we taught them how to listen to each other, to make apologies when needed, and to work through their misunderstandings.

The time we invested talking with them while they were little formed the foundation for deep communication when they were older. We discussed the pros and cons of college, of self-employment, of various occupations. We spent time in serious discussion about business potentials, purchasing their own vehicles, and building versus buying their own first homes. We discussed issues like indebtedness, civic responsibilities, and voting.

Girls were a big topic of conversation as they got older. They both believed that God wanted them to marry some day and carry on the legacy of a Christ-centered home. "Father, how do you know which girl is right? She might have a pretty face and dress attractively, but what if she is a sloppy housekeeper?" We discussed God's principles and how they apply to finding a life mate. We talked about life in general. We rehearsed and reinforced godly principles until they were theirs.

Time to play together, time to work as a team, and time to talk as the closest of confidants—all this interaction gave abundant opportunity to do what the Bible calls nurturing and admonishing. To nurture is to encourage somebody to grow, develop, thrive, and be successful. We did this for our boys by affirming them with words and looks, by hugging and kissing them, holding their hands when we went for walks, and tucking them in bed at night. All this gentle affirmation encourages them that they have value, that they are treasured, that you believe in them and are there for them. To admonish means to rebuke mildly but earnestly, to advise, to caution, and to warn.

SMASH!

Childrearing is impossible for any of us to do without heavenly guidance, and I found it was often as much a learning experience for me as it was for them. One day I had just finished a phone conversation when Matthew strode through the back door with a troubled expression on his face.

"What's up, Matthew?" I queried, while my mind still processed the phone call I had just finished.

"Father," Matthew spoke hesitantly, "could you come out to the garage with me? I need to show you something."

Matthew was strangely silent as he led me out to the garage, around to the back of the truck, and pointed to a smashed rear tail light. My eye took in the situation at a glance. Matthew had backed the truck into the garage and failed to notice that the handle of the snow blower was protruding farther into his pathway than usual. Failed to notice, that is, until he heard the crunching of the plastic part.

Suddenly, I was irritated. *That stupid kid,* I grumbled inwardly. *Can't he pay attention to where he is backing up?* But just as quickly, God brought another picture to my mind—the picture of me in the driver's seat of that very truck backing into the mailbox while I was out plowing the road and causing the identical damage to the truck that Matthew had just inflicted.

Thanks for the reminder, Lord! I realize that without God, I would have the same tendency many other fathers have to chew out their youngsters for their mistakes and leave them feeling wounded and ashamed. Some fathers would even go so far as to pay for the broken tail light but never repair the broken spirit of their offspring. That is not nurturing and admonishing. That is alienating and crippling.

I glanced at Matthew. His head was down, and he was watching for my reaction out of the corner of his eye. I put my hand on his back.

"Well, Matthew," I began, "it looks like you have just made the same mistake I made some time ago. Makes you feel kind of foolish, doesn't it?"

Matthew looked up, and his eyes met mine. I could read relief written there. You see, when our children learn that we mess up too, they feel better!

We went back into the house and talked it through. As Matthew realized that he wasn't going to get a tongue-lashing or the cold-shoulder treatment for his mistake, he opened up. We talked about how mistakes happen in life and that adults must take responsibility for them. We called the parts store and found out that the light would cost seventy-five dollars to replace.

"Matthew," I said, "seventy-five dollars is a lot of money for you at your stage of life. But this is an excellent opportunity for you to learn how to take responsibility for your own actions. If you don't learn that now, and you make a careless mistake that involves you in an accident, you will spend thousands of dollars in increased auto insurance premiums. If I always carry the weight of fixing everything, you won't have the opportunity to learn."

It was a tough lesson for Matthew, but he learned it well. He learned to accept himself even when he made mistakes but to still take responsibility for those mistakes. Rarely is there a successful person who hasn't had to build success upon the failures of the past, and this is what I wanted Matthew to learn. This is nurturing and admonishing. It takes time. It requires a denial of my flesh. It demands being both tender and firm. But it is worth it. My son's spirit remained intact while he grew in maturity, and today I see the evidence in a successful young man.

I turned from the window to ponder this special room once again. This time, my gaze wandered over the bookshelf. Each familiar title aroused memories of shared moments. Reading character-building stories and talking them over together was so rewarding. A well-used volume of the Scriptures captivated my thoughts. "Yes, Lord," I mused. "That volume captures the essence and cornerstone of building men."

True connection

You see, all of our effort toward building real men would be fruitless if we failed to connect them with their Creator. It would be like teaching them to sail and sending them out to sea without a compass, or giving them flight lessons but never training them to tune in to the control tower. The real aim of parenting is to train our young people to dwell in the shadow of the Most High—not under our shadow. It is to connect them with Him who is always a safe Guide and Companion. It is to bring them to the experience of knowing and doing the will of God for themselves—not merely because Dad says so.

We didn't restrict instruction about the Christian walk to any certain time or place. Every activity afforded an opportunity to teach by example, by instruction, by leading in prayer and action. At the same time, we also structured our daily routine around personal and family worship. Those times were set in concrete, so to speak.

When we first moved to the wilderness, Sally was the priest of our home. She carried the responsibility for the spiritual nurture and guidance of our two boys. As time went on, God began to convict me that this was my duty, my God-given role. At first, I resisted. Something inside of me just didn't want to make that investment. After wrestling for some time, I yielded to God and picked up that role. I have never regretted it!

When our boys were very young, we joined them for their personal worship and helped them draw conclusions and apply the lessons to their own lives. Once they could read on their own, I questioned them on what they read and what the application was for their lives today. My questions helped them learn to seek personal application and lessons to guide them throughout the day. We encouraged them to study those issues that they were facing in their daily lives so that they could begin to understand God's will. "It doesn't matter what Father or Mother think. It doesn't matter what they think. What really matters is what God thinks."

Our family worships were scheduled for eight o'clock in the morning and eight o'clock in the evening. I had participated in other family worships that were tedious, dry, and boring. I didn't want worships to be that way in our home, so we had worked hard to make family worship the highlight of the day—interesting, full of life, and relevant. We all met around the dining room table and after singing a hymn, we knelt for a short prayer. Usually we used the Bible or another character-building book as a catalyst for our discussions. We started by taking turns reading a paragraph and summarizing the main ideas presented and, more important, anything that struck a responsive chord personally with the reader. Anyone was then free to comment. Through this avenue, the Holy Spirit opened up deep conversation about applying these principles to our practical experience. After fifteen or twenty minutes of reading and discussing, we closed with prayer and hugs all around.

We have come to value the tremendous benefit of this kind of participation. Our boys have become very comfortable talking about spiritual things and articulating their views and questions—as well as sharing their struggles, temptations, and victories.

WORTH IT ALL!

It was quite a reflection that evening, just my God and me, as I thought about all the time, thought, energy, and prayer I had invested in those two boys. And now they are gone to their own homes, and life will never be quite the same. Was it worth it?

Well, the other weekend, Sally and I spent the weekend visiting with Matthew, Andrew, and their wives. Sunday afternoon I was ready to head home. I had things to do Monday morning. The boys tried to talk me into staying longer, but we'd had a good visit and there was no reason to delay my departure any longer, or so I thought.

"Don't go until I show you something!" Matthew interjected.

"All right," I responded, "but don't take all day."

He returned with the mystery item hidden behind his back. I waited expectantly, but he just eyed Andrew, who nodded. All of a sudden, Matthew's hand came out with a coil of rope and both of them jumped on me. I was completely tied up amid shrieks of laughter, belatedly becoming aware that my boys, grown men with their own homes, were telling me in a way impossible to mistake that they still wanted and loved time with their father. The bond between all six of us is real and strong.

Yes, they are now men—real men, standing on their own under God. I have become a grandpa. Matthew and Angela have a son named Nathan. Andrew and Sarah have two sons: Landon and Jesse. They have picked up the legacy God gave me and are carrying it to new depths. Was it worth it? It was worth every moment of time, every denial of my desires, every change I had to make, and every cross I had to bear. I would do it all over again and a thousand times more to reap the harvest of joy I now have. I now have no regrets, and best of all, in my heart is the deep satisfaction that every father can share of having partnered with God for the purpose of building men. Will you do the same for your children?

CHAPTER 10
BUILDING MEN
Questions to Consider for Personal Inventory or Group Discussion

1. What am I building? A business? An empire? A life for myself? Or am I building men and women?
2. What kind of characters do my children possess? Are they firm to follow principle and say no to compromise, or do they fold under peer pressure?
3. Looking back over this past week, how much time did I devote to my children?
4. When was the last time I entered into a simple game such as tag or dominoes or read a book with them?
5. When was the last time I went on a special outing that meant something to them?
6. Does my home run like a well-oiled machine?
7. When was the last time I worked on a simple task or special project with my children and let them know I appreciate their efforts?
8. Do I go "outside my own box" to meet the needs and desires of my children?
9. What are my conversations like with my children—lively and interesting, or bored and strained?
10. Do I conduct regular family worship in my home? Would my children say they look forward to it or that they dread it?
11. What am I doing to prepare my children for real life—relationships, occupation, operating a home efficiently?

A Friend for Me

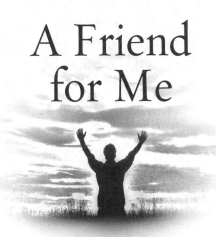

There is a friend that sticketh closer than a brother.
—Proverbs 18:24

Most of the men I talk with have friendships—lots of them—through the course of their lives. Yet they have never found that one *special* friend, the friend that sticks closer than a brother, the way the book of Proverbs describes it. These men are solid, good men, but in this category, they feel empty because their lives are not marked by even one such friendship. I used to wonder about this type of friend. I often wondered, like many of the men I talked to, if such a friend really existed. And if they did, would there ever be one for me? It's only as I have aged and been able to look back through the years that I have begun to understand the real dynamics of male friendship amid the ebb and flow of life.

MISCHIEF MAKERS

Bill was my first friend. I can still picture the neighborhood that formed the nucleus of my life as a seven-year-old on South Sanders Street in Appleton, Wisconsin. Bill lived across the street and three doors down. I don't remember how we met, but Bill became my first real friend. We rode our bikes together or roller-skated, when we weren't out exploring.

Bill's house was at the corner, and on the other side of his house was River View Country Club. It was an exclusive place with manicured fairways and putting greens, but what interested us were the parts of the property golfers rarely saw—the brush, the creeks cutting through steep ravines, the river, and the thick woods interspersed along the course. Here was a world containing all that boys could desire. We made forts in the trees and played for hours on end. Other friends joined us, and I still remember the five of us—two Bills, two Jims, and a lone Butch, jumping on our Tarzan trees. What? You never played Tarzan? You don't know the fun you were missing. Near our tree fort, there were some young aspen trees. Three or four of us would leap out of the tree fort into the aspen tree and climb as high as we could. Our combined weight would bend the flexible tree over until it touched the ground. Then three of us would let go and the tree would whip up, carrying the final member of our party on a wildly exciting journey.

Looking back on it now, I realize it was a game fraught with danger. Perhaps it is just as well our parents didn't know what we were doing, but isn't this the very essence of life for most boys? The thrill of danger and the spirit of adventure merely heighten the enjoyment of the activity. I am so thankful I grew up in a day when society still realized that swimming in a forbidden pond or, dare I say, "trespassing" on the private golf club were not signs of juvenile delinquency but simply the thoughtless expression of normal boyhood in all its exuberance.

The boyish inability to foresee problems and prevent them often leads to unexpected consequences, and I was no exception. For example, whenever I could, I caught frogs in the creek by the golf course and brought them home to my makeshift aquarium, fashioned from a large metal washtub fitted with a lid. It was with no little pride that I surveyed my kingdom, numbering fourteen frogs of various sizes. How large my collection might have grown will never be known. At this point I either failed to properly affix the lid or it was somehow jarred loose. At any rate, my father discovered the escapees as he headed down the stairs in the dark and felt the body of my largest and most dearly beloved bullfrog squish between his toes. It was, as I recall, a delicate parental moment, and it ended my frog collection.

Yes, boys like danger. For them, it is almost like salt on their food—it just adds flavor to any situation. The golf course was like that for us. We loved playing there, and the fact that we didn't belong there just added to the excitement. The maintenance men at the golf club occasionally spotted us and came to chase us off. We'd run for cover, and soon a whole new game was born. They were the enemy, and we had to escape.

We didn't have names for the men, so we just called them the truck man and the tractor man after the vehicles they drove. They became the almost-perfect enemy—always wanting to get rid of us, but never as malicious or scary as to take away the fun. I truly believe they even enjoyed some of our interactions—like the time they snuck up on our tree fort. We didn't discover them until too late, and we all bolted out of the tree and blazed a trail down a ravine we'd never traveled before. Our path was strewn with thorns, briers, and those cockleburs that grab hold of your clothes or hair and hitchhike along with you.

I remember what a sorry sight we were when we emerged on the opposite bank of the ravine from our pursuers, muddy, covered in burs, with torn clothes and scratched skin, and those men stood there and laughed and laughed. They probably still enjoy telling the story, and we didn't begrudge them their victory.

Bill and I were similar—shy and a bit withdrawn, yet full of childish mischief. However, we did more than just monkey business together. We walked to school together, played ball, and flew kites, just like other young boys. We were bosom buddies from age seven until about fourteen, when my parents decided to move to a new section of town. I didn't see Bill much after that. I didn't understand it at the time, but he passed out of my life—a dear, dear friend, lost not to a fight or misunderstanding but to circumstances.

Vroom, vroom

The thing about life is that it keeps on going, even when we suffer a loss. In our new home, I soon became acquainted with another young man my age who lived across the street. I first noticed Mike when he started up his motorcycle—a 175cc Honda. This caught my eye because I was the proud owner of a 150cc Suzuki—my first motorcycle.

We met one day on the street and were soon cruising the roads together. We drove to High Cliff State Park and explored all the back roads. We enjoyed the dirt trails of Playman Park, where we'd pop wheelies and see who could hold one the longest. We were adventurers. We teamed up with two other guys who had motorcycles. Dick had a Ducati, a big old noisy bike. I don't think they even make that model anymore. Jerry rode a Harley Davidson. Our group met on Sundays, and we'd explore new parts of a world that was just opening up to us now that we had wheels. We'd stop in at Murphy's and feed coins into the jukebox, drink root beers, chat, and occasionally flirt with the girls. Mike and I drove to school together, and when I started dating Sally, he and I would meet her on the road and serve as her motorcycle escort to school. It was a wonderful time in the 1960s, a real-life "Happy Days" setting. But events would soon alter these friendships as well.

Oops!

One day, I found myself stuck behind a student driver who was obviously scared to death and very hesitant. I, as usual, was in a hurry and so was following too closely when she slammed on her brakes at a railroad crossing. Now you are probably aware that the foot brake on a motorcycle is for your rear brake and the hand brake is for the front. Well, as I jammed on both brakes in a panic, my foot slipped off the rear brake pedal. My front tire locked up, and I was catapulted over her car to land on her hood looking in the window. It was a strange sensation, and if she was scared before, she was terrified then. I was unhurt and, thanks to better construction of motor vehicles in those days, nothing was damaged other than a few scratches on my bike, so we both went on our way.

I was shaken, but only for a few minutes. After all, I reasoned, "Anyone can have one accident," and things went all right until I went out after a rain. Once more I was in a rush and following too closely when a dog ran out in front of the car ahead of me. Again I found myself braking hard to avoid a collision, but on the wet road my bike skidded and I was forced to let go of the bike as it slid under the car. Only my grabbing hold of the back bumper prevented me from following the bike. All in all, I was lucky—very lucky—a few scrapes on the bike and a few more on my hide were the extent of the damage.

Now both these accidents were, in essence, my fault, although the police weren't notified and no insurance claims were filed. However, they did little to take away my self-confidence. I simply resolved to be more careful in the future. My mother's view was different, and it found expression one Sunday morning when I headed out for a ride before meeting up with the guys.

As I was saying goodbye, she insisted, "Son, put your helmet on."

"Oh, Mom, come on, nobody is wearing them."

"Put your helmet on or give me your keys."

I knew she meant it, so I reluctantly put on my helmet. About an hour later I was headed back into town with a little time to spare before meeting the guys, so I decided to pull into the office complex just around the next curve because they had a wonderful little trout pond behind the building and I enjoyed just taking in the peaceful scene. I slowed up, preparing to turn right into the parking lot.

I didn't know it, but I wasn't the only one who thought this was a great day for a motorcycle ride and another rider was coming up rapidly behind me, planning to pass me on the right! I turned toward the parking lot just as he came alongside, and we collided with a stunning impact. I was thrown through the air and hit the curb headfirst. When I could take stock of my situation, I found I had once again escaped serious injury, but my helmet was cracked right down the middle!

After this incident, my mother convinced me to sell the bike and get a car. I ended up with a black 1960 Chevy Impala with big fins in the back. Since I no longer had a motorcycle, I didn't fit in with the gang anymore, and we just didn't see each other much after that. I never quite understood how the loss of a motorcycle so altered our friendships that they died away, but it did.

By this time I was working for a Standard Oil gas station, pumping gas and doing minor repairs, and it was here I met Dave. He'd come in for gas when he got off work at the hardware store, and we struck up a friendship. One fall day, he asked if I'd like to go deer hunting with him. I said, "I'd love to," and a new friendship was born.

DAREDEVILS

The place he liked to go hunting was ninety minutes away, and to get up there and hike in before daylight meant we'd have to leave Appleton about three thirty in the morning. We left early and hunted all day for the elusive twelve-point buck of our dreams. Then we stopped at a drive-in to slug down a couple burgers, fries, and a shake before returning home. Then we'd do it all over again in a few days.

We became each other's sidekick. We hunted together, we double dated, and we drag-raced our cars. By that point, I had a Pontiac Le-Mans Convertible and Dave had a Dodge Charger 440 with a HEMI-Hertz shift. Those were muscle cars, and we were young, reckless, and footloose. Tom soon joined our group with his Pontiac Grand Prix. It was a 421 with three—that's right, one, two, three carbs—and was that car fast! Off the line or top end, there was nothing that could touch it. I was with him once when we raced someone with a Mustang 390 with a four-barrel carb. We buried the speedometer at 140 miles per hour and left them in the dust.

Fired with the illusion of youthful immortality, we were hopeless daredevils. Once we raced each other from Shawano to Appleton, Wisconsin, some forty-five miles away with the loser paying for everyone's drinks. I had the slowest car of the trio, but I was determined to win. I passed more than forty cars in a row doing a hundred miles an hour. I just barely glimpsed the state trooper in the middle of the row, but he wanted to live and didn't dare follow.

I had everything I could have asked for: two good friends, a fast car, and a pretty girl. Then high school ended, and we all had to grow up. I went off to college, Dave became an apprentice electrician at a foundry, and Tom joined the military. We never really saw much of each other after that. Occasionally our paths cross, but college ended all our close friendships. Once more, I wondered why this happens . . . but not for long.

KABOOM!

In college, I became buddies with my roommates, and we teamed up to rent a four-bedroom house. Let me assure you, if you haven't lived with four college guys, if you haven't tried to cook, clean, and do laundry with four college guys, you've missed the education of a lifetime. It was never dull or boring!

One night the four of us, Tom, John, Lynn, and I, stopped off for a little refreshment on the way home. As it turned out, it was a little too much refreshment! We picked up a couple of frozen pizzas. Being the first one in the house, I turned on the gas oven but didn't take the time to light it. Instead, I just ran upstairs to the bathroom. After about five minutes, I noticed the strong smell of gas.

"John," I yelled down. "Light that stove!"

Well, the next thing I knew there was a huge B-A-N-G! The entire house shook with the impact, and I ran downstairs to find that John had been blown against the wall opposite the stove. Miraculously, he was not badly injured. His hair was a little singed from flash burns, and he was wondering what had happened to him. The oven was a bomb waiting for some unfortunate to set it off, and the fact he'd gotten away unhurt seemed impossible and therefore funny—at least in our inebriated state! Laughing, we helped him up, and he put the pizzas in the oven while we had another beer. When the pizzas were done, we sat down to our feast, but they were the worst pizzas I have ever eaten. Everybody else thought so too. It took us quite a while to realize that after his near-death experience, John had forgotten to remove the plastic wrapper before baking them.

These were my friends for those special college years. All three attended my wedding in 1972. I was the first of the group to tie the knot, and then we graduated and never really saw each other after that. John and Lynn found wives and married, but not Tom, who tragically died about fifteen years later. You know, whenever we get together, we reenter those glory days. We reminisce about our favorite tales and adventures, laugh a lot for all we shared, cry a little over all we've lost, especially Tom, and in the end realize that we shared a very special time together, a unique period of our lives in which our hearts beat as one. However, life moved on and so did we. We entered different chapters in our lives—chapters in which we didn't fit seamlessly into each others' lives anymore.

Don't any stick?

I used to wonder, why don't these relationships stick better? Why do none of them seem to be close forever? All my relationships seemed transitional, and I began asking my siblings, my parents, extended family, co-workers, and friends, and every one of them told stories of bonding and then going their separate ways. Oh, they all had fond memories, but rarely a deep and lasting bond. Sure, in most of these cases, we still consider ourselves friends, still exchange Christmas or birthday cards, still enjoy a chance meeting or a rare phone call, but we've each moved on, changed occupations, interests, hobbies, even belief systems, and in so doing we've left off our old ways and embraced new things. Somehow, without even a conscious thought, the old camaraderie is gone and new relationships develop.

It would be nearly impossible to maintain all the relationships you've been privileged to develop from childhood onward. This isn't a rationalization for lost friendships, but the plain fact that we only have so much time we can invest in friendships.

Jesus may have had twelve friends who were closer than most to Him, but among them only Peter, James, and John were truly His best friends. It seems that even our Lord, when constrained by human flesh, could not manage to maintain twelve "best" friends.

In looking back over my early life, these were the boys I counted as friends: my early childhood buddies, Bill, Butch, Jimmy, Bill; my motorcycle guys, Mike, Dick, and Jerry; my later high-school sidekicks, Dave and Tom; my college roommates, John, Tom, and Lynn. That's twelve in all, but it doesn't begin to mention all the guys I was a friend with casually in Scouts, sports, and at school. And let's not forget the half dozen girls I dated before Sally!

But this is just my youth. Later there were Paul and Ethel, the wonderful people who introduced me to the Bible. My life changed as I came to know about God, and when I gave up partying and drinking, I became connected with a whole new group of interesting people. There was Gary, who became my hunting and camping buddy, and several couples, Mike and Annette, Tom and Lana, Chuck and Mary, as well as Bill and Eleanor. Several ministers became good friends—Bob, Jim,

Dan, Vern, and Jerry. But how could I manage to maintain friendships—close friendships—with half a hundred people spread all over the country?

SHIFTING SANDS

So, where am I going with all this? Simply that I have discovered that there are three basic types of friends. First, there are friends for a *season*, which was what my first friend, Bill, was. We were neighborhood buddies as long as we lived near each other. My college friends were friends for a season. You enjoy the season, the period of life that has brought you together. These are not bad friendships. They are formed with nice people, good people. But life changes, friends change, and you move on. This doesn't demean the people you were friends with. No indeed, for your life has been enriched and shaped by those who share this season with you, and you carry in your being not just the memories but the very essence of the things you gained, learned, and experienced with and through them.

Second, there are friends for a *reason*. My motorcycling friend, Mike, was this type of friend. Our commonality of interest brought us together. Today I doubt any of us are still out cruising the roads of High Cliff State Park. The reason we were drawn together is no longer there. The same is true of Dave and Tom with our muscle cars. None of us are out chasing girls or drinking ourselves silly. I still see Tom occasionally. He owns his own car lot, and we'll reminisce or go out to eat. We still exchange Christmas cards, and he remains a dear, dear person and in a sense a friend, but for the most part and in both of our lives, our relationship has served its purpose. Its reason for being has faded and new lives have been formed. Each of us is like a beach scoured by shifting tides, storms, and wind. Each change, no matter how small, has altered our landscape year by year until dramatic changes have occurred. Reflecting back over the seasons of time and reasons for my friendships, my heart is warmed by all the influences friends have brought into my life. Some made me a better person. Some involved me in more mischief. Some saw me through a period of growth. Others were just there, at the same time and the same life transitions, and we were blessed mutually to have traveled for a time together. I have learned too late in life, as we human beings tend to do, that I can treasure and savor each state, each wave, each journey of life and every person brought into my life that I can call a friend.

MY DEEPER DESIRE

But what about that one special friend, the one the Bible speaks of as sticking closer than a brother?[1] A "friend [that] loveth at all times,"[2] a friend who is there for you through periods of adversity and triumph and unchanged by either? What about someone whose heart is in harmony with my own and not in my life just for a reason or a season, but always there, caring, regardless of where I live, what my occupation is, whether my belief system changes, or if our shared activities fall by the wayside, someone who is truly closer than a brother?

I used to wonder if I would ever find such a friend and never did until the fourth decade of my life. For most of us, this desire for a "forever friend" remains an elusive, unfulfilled dream. Even our Lord and Savior found when the crisis came that not only did His friends forsake Him, but even the closest of the close. Peter denied Him! In the end, He was alone! Don't be shocked or dumbfounded if at the end of your life, there turns out to be no friend for you who sticks closer than a brother. Jesus, John the Baptist, Elisha, Daniel, Isaiah, Jeremiah, Moses, and Joseph—not one has a history of such a friend.

But a minority did find such companions. Paul had Luke, who, even when Paul was jailed, was always with him looking after his welfare and health. David had Jonathan, who laid down his crown and future for him. In nonbiblical times, Luther had Melancthon, and John Wesley had his brother, Charles. We are truly fortunate if we find the same.

In examining my own life and heart as I write this chapter, I must say that my wife is my most intimate companion. I say this not because of some principle that your wife *should* be your closest companion,

---

1. See Proverbs 18:24.
2. Proverbs 17:17.

but from reality. I'd be willing to die for her instantly. Yet, there remains in the human heart—at least in this man's heart—the desire to have someone to die with, to die beside . . . another man, a soul mate to share my heart, purpose, God-given direction, determination, and desires.

SOUL MATE

When I moved to the wilderness, I left behind all I had known, including my friends. I had no great expectation of finding that one true, faithful friend in the sparsely populated North Fork. Yet, if I have learned anything about the God I serve, it is that He is the God of the impossible. In His great wisdom, He brought a friend into my life and, in so doing, brought me a friendship that was so fulfilling in so many different ways that it became unique in my experience.

This man entered wholeheartedly into the same desires for his family that I had for mine. He wrestled with many of the same personal struggles and failings that I did. Together we could speak of things no one else understood, of spiritual battles no one we knew was engaged in. We could have fun together and experience some grand adventures—some fraught with danger like the time my friend nearly died on a mountainside or the time both of us were severely hypothermic after a frigid-water canoeing accident. These things alone would bind our hearts together, but in time we also began to work jointly, teaching others the very things we had learned as we worked to restore our marriages and our families.

This doesn't mean there was perfect harmony between us or that we always saw things the same, for we certainly didn't in all areas. In fact, it would be most unusual to find someone with whom we are in complete agreement on every issue, but we were resolved to allow each other the freedom to follow God as his conscience dictated and enjoyed many years of working together, socializing together, and most of all growing together as we encouraged each other in our individual walks with God. As we did things together, our families would run across areas where there were sincere differences of opinion—not on areas related to salvation, but those involving the day-to-day practical application of Christianity in the home and in society.

For example, my family enjoyed reading a set of nature stories and found them to be good character-building books. We were a little surprised when my friend's family objected to them because the author used personification to portray the animal characters in the story. I'm not here to debate the rightness or wrongness of the issue. For them, it was an issue. We didn't agree on this or on a half dozen other non-moral issues.

DISTURBING DOUBTS

Little agitations and slights began to fester, and my natural inclination was to think of my friend as too rigid or too conservative while he tended to see me as too liberal, too compromising. Almost imperceptibly, attitudes changed. They just couldn't understand why we didn't see their valid concern and vice-versa, and suddenly, where before we'd always encouraged each other, a little seed of doubt and concern regarding the other and their spiritual growth sprang up. When this happens on another issue and then another, you begin to see each other less often, and when you do, it is with an undercurrent of worry that you may run into yet another conflict.

Now I believe it is possible for sincere Christians to differ on their evaluation of an issue and yet both remain sincere Christians. However, I don't believe that any of us has a God-given right or duty to dictate to another what they should or shouldn't do in any nonsalvation issue. Moreover, such conflicts arise in Christian circles over virtually every area of life: clothes, entertainment, food, Bible versions, theology, philosophy, preaching and worship style, music, and even decorating.

The solution to such situations is not pulling apart from each other. Rather, we need to spend sufficient time with each other allowing freedom to disagree on nonmoral issues. We need to give each other time to grow in our own perceptions and understandings of the issues, remembering the shared values and ideals that drew us together in the first place. When this happens, we can once more encourage each other and leave the areas on which we disagree to God. In our case, however, at the very time our relationship was increasingly stressed by minor conflicts and in need of time invested in each other, the demands of a growing ministry increasingly limited that time.

When we got together, business demanded attention and the easy, casual camaraderie we'd enjoyed for so many years faded. Conflicts lurked beneath the surface, and when efforts at addressing them were rebuffed, we committed the cardinal error of allowing them to remain unresolved, perhaps hoping they'd work themselves out.

Friend or frienemy?

Ironically, the dam broke in an area many have honestly wrestled with: final authority over our young adults' lives in choosing a life partner. One believes that after counseling and coaching them, they are at liberty before God and man to decide whom and when they marry. Another believes that without the parents' complete permission they are not at liberty to marry.

Regardless of how you line up on this somewhat sensitive issue, it was the resulting attitudes, approaches, and actions taken that brought in the flood of hurt and distress that drowned the relationship.

Once one side or the other takes these steps, the way is prepared for pride of opinion and jealousy of influence to find their sneaky little way in. These rascals usually deal the final blow to the friendship.

It is impossible for me to evaluate my friend's motives, and I won't pretend to have a full understanding of his actions. I'll say only that he, in conjunction with some others, soon launched into a series of actions that I found to be extremely hurtful to me and my family—as well as a violation of the golden rule of relationships that says, " 'But if your brother wrongs you, go and have it out with him at once—just between the two of you. If he will listen to you, you have won him back as your brother.' "[3]

Many people have asked me to detail my friend's actions and I have refused to do so, other than to state that those who need to know and are involved in the situation already know the facts. I think my friend acted in the way he felt was best from his perspective. However, my perception of his behavior is another matter. While I can only speculate upon his motives, I know what I experi-

---

3. Matthew 18:15, Phillips.

enced and his actions were, to me, a monstrous betrayal of all I had thought we once held dear. My friend, my confidant, and my partner in ministry turned on me. He may have felt he had no choice, no other option. He may feel he did only what was right in his eyes. Nevertheless, I experienced his actions as a sell-out of our relationship. He twisted the principles of religious liberty and individuality that I hold precious to give the appearance that I was going astray. He who once stood by my side became my accuser. My friend became my "frienemy."

Oh, for words adequate to convey the heartbreak of this situation! The feelings of grief that wash over the human soul are so oppressive that they make one physically ill. I suspect some of you understand not only my agony, but also your own. If you've experienced it, you understand! Life's not always fair. Moses had his betrayers in Korah, Dathan, Abiram, and his own dear siblings; Joseph was betrayed and sold by his brothers; and Jesus had His Judas. If you've tasted of the same, you're in good company. I have come to see that God can work any situation, no matter how bitter, for good. That is what He has done for me during this dark, dark time in my life.

In my agony, late one night, I wrote this poem as I poured my heart out to God.

"No Friend for Me?"

Lord, You called and I came.
You said, "Leave your homeland for me,
Your business, your companions."
I said, "Lord, I'll have *no friend* for me."

Lord, You said, "Make me the Lord of your life,
The center of your marriage,
The nucleus of your family."
"Yes, Lord, but what about a *friend* for me?"

Lord, You called me to share the Good News with others,
To bring them into my home,

To teach them your ways,
To Help your people grow.
"Yes, Lord, but I have *no friend* for me!"

Lord, You asked me to leave my mountain solitude,
To give my life for your people,
To preach Your message,
To restore Your multitude.
"But, Lord, still *no friend* for me!"

Lord, Your program has worked.
Your people are returning,
Marriages are healing.
Families are responding.
"Lord, how come *no friend* for me?"

"Jim, I trod the winepress alone,
Of the people there was *none* for Me.
I healed the sick, opened eyes for the blind,
Cured the leper and set the captive free,
And I wondered that there was *none for me!*

"But Lord, is there *no friend* for me?"
"Jim, how about *Me?*"

LIGHT IN THE DARKNESS

It brought me a lot of comfort to know the Lord would be my Friend always, would never sell me out. But God didn't stop there. He went on and provided the very someone I needed right then. This friend knew everyone involved. He understood the circumstances, and when I called him, he came. He was there for me throughout the trials and stood by my side when others abandoned me. He saw through the gossip, the innuendo, the misinformation, the rumors, and the false characterizations. He became a real soul mate.

Just when I was thanking the Lord for one friend, He sent ten! Ten men emerged to stand by me in this hour of crisis. They allied themselves with me when things looked the darkest; when to any worldly view such a connection would only bring them possible reproach. In so doing, they taught me a lot about friendships, about being there in good times and bad, of *being there . . . period!* The true in heart emerge amidst the darkness, just when the false are showing their true colors.

I came to see that God was allowing my life and my friendships to be sifted in the crucible of adversity, and in these ten men I found friends I could bare my soul with and they would bear me up in cooperation with my Lord and Savior. They helped me, but not by attacking my former friend. In fact, they universally counseled against such a course because they were men of principle. Their loyalty was unquestioned, yet they retained their own ideas and let me know if they thought I was wrong. They unselfishly gave of themselves as they bore with me my burden of pain. They were courageous in the face of apparent defeat. They were sensitive and not afraid to be vulnerable. Their freely shared affection was like a healing balm to me. On top of it all, they share the same values I do. These ten men proved themselves worthy of my trust and affection.

I also discovered in my sons, Matthew and Andrew, now men themselves, an inexhaustible source of inspiration and principled courage. In spite of personal assaults, they never sought revenge or entered into mud slinging.

BEST THING IN THE WORST WAY

At the time of this writing more than four years have passed since our friendship dissolved, and I was recently asked to summarize this dark time in my life. I can honestly say that it was the best thing that ever happened to me in the worst possible way. The evil perpetrated on us, God used for good. Experiences like this will either lift you up in Christ or crush you. If these fires of affliction are allowed to do their work, the dross—that is, the impurities—are burned out of your character, refining you as gold.[4]

Christ was betrayed twice the night He was arrested and placed on trial—once by Judas and once by Peter. Christ's heart was drawn out in

---

4. See Job 23:10; 28:1.

love toward both men. How could He give up on either one of them? One of them severed forever the possibility of reconciliation. The other was restored into the closest bonds of friendship. It can happen. So I hope it will be somewhere, sometime, with this friendship I have lost. Only time will tell if we shall ever be close friends again, and I dedicate this chapter to the one who was "a friend for me," and if willing, could be once more.

CHAPTER 11

A FRIEND FOR ME

Questions to Consider for Personal Inventory or Group Discussion

1. As I look back over my life, what kinds of friendships do I identify?
   a. Friends for a season
   b. Friends for a reason
   c. Deep, lasting friendships
2. When I disagree with a friend, do I pull apart and withdraw?
3. Am I allowing conflicts to remain unresolved?
4. Can I disagree agreeably?
5. Can I value and respect my friend's differences?
6. Can I give him freedom to grow with God in his own unique way?
7. If a relationship breaks down, do I guard my friend's reputation while looking for solutions?
8. What is God bringing to my mind that I can do to improve or repair a friendship?
9. What kind of a friend would others say that I am?

SECTION THREE

Defeating the Defeaters

None who trust their Coach need fear the defeaters!

CHAPTER 12
TOUCHING THE TABOO

CHAPTER 13
JUMBLED PRIORITIES

CHAPTER 14
MEN OF POWER

Touching
the Taboo

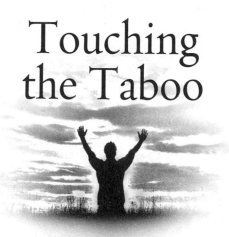

He that covereth his sins shall not prosper:
but whoso confesseth and forsaketh them shall have mercy.
—Proverbs 28:13

"Jim, I've had an unsettling experience I want to tell you about," Bill, an employee at a Christian university, said over the phone. "As you know, in my job, I am responsible for the university's Internet access, and recently I installed a program that tracks the use of pornography on the Web. I didn't expect to find much, so I was more than a little taken aback when it showed one-third of the male students accessing pornography on a regular basis. Some of these students were actually in training to become church pastors. But I was even more alarmed to find several faculty members doing the same thing, and some of these were department heads! Now, I'm not talking about inadvertent access to a site for a moment or two, which is almost inevitable while surfing the Web in an unrestricted environment. These men were spending a significant portion of their online time viewing pornography—some as much as twenty-five hours per week!"

"What did you do?" I asked.

"I went to the university president."

"And what was his reaction?"

"He was appalled."

"He should have been."

"Oh, not with the offenders, but with me. He interrogated me for three hours to see what I'd been up to, and told me I was to stop all such monitoring and never to start it up again. Furthermore, I was to destroy any records created by my invasion of privacy, and if I ever mentioned this to anyone, I was history!"

My friend is hardly alone in his discovery. I'm sure system managers from most companies could tell similar stories, but what makes his tale so tragic is that this happened at a Christian university. In his book *Men's Secret Wars,*[1] Patrick Means reveals a confidential survey of evangelical pastors and church lay leaders. Sixty-four percent of these Christian leaders confirm that they are struggling with sexual addiction, including the use of pornography, compulsive masturbation, or other secret sexual activity.

What God made is good!

God had a purpose when He made men masculine. He gave man distinctive drives to motivate him to be the provider and protector of his family while regarding their needs above his own. His courage, integrity, and purpose combined with real heart enable him to connect emotionally with his wife and children in healthy, wholesome relationship. The culmination of his unselfish affection is expressed as he unites physically with his wife in an atmosphere of warmth, acceptance, and intimacy. What God created is beautiful, pure, and holy, and He rejoices in it.

God designed physical intimacy to work well in one context only—and no other. That context is a committed, loving marriage between one man and one woman.[2] Sexual expression in any other context is sinful and separates us from both God and our loved ones.[3] Is this because God is narrow-minded or straight-laced? Not any more than is the automobile manufacturer who recommends you only put unleaded gasoline in your fuel tank. If you have ever made the mistake of filling up with diesel or leaded fuel, you know it just doesn't work

---

1. Patrick Means, *Men's Secret Wars* (Grand Rapids, Mich.: Fleming H. Revell, 1999).

2. See Genesis 2:24, 25; Hebrews 13:4; 1 Corinthians 7:7–9.

3. See 1 Corinthians 6:13–20; 1 Peter 2:11; Romans 1:24–32; Isaiah 59:1, 2.

well. Your engine smokes, sputters, and misfires. It never purrs the way it should.

Even so, people don't function well without loving relationships with God and others. Our enemy is always offering substitutes, and lust is one of his counterfeits for love.

UNDER ATTACK

The problem is that lust in the soul is like diesel in an unleaded fuel tank. It makes your life smoke, sputter, and misfire. It destroys from within all that is truly valuable. I have yet to meet a man whose life runs well with lust. When sexual drive is viewed as a need that must be satisfied, it becomes an idol. It takes priority over all else. It leads a man to abuse himself or to sacrifice his wife—or worse yet, his children—upon the altar of lust. After all that, lust not only fails to deliver what it promised, but it also most surely destroys what is needed—a safe environment with loving, secure relationships. What God intended to be beautiful becomes twisted, ugly, and destructive.

In the place of finding satisfaction, the man finds shame. He hides. He isolates. He wouldn't dare admit that he struggles with these things because of the stigma he feels. The very drive that God instilled in him to move him toward a deep, healthy relationship is turned around to isolate him from the very thing he needs.

Perhaps that is why Satan has worked so untiringly to pervert this gift. He knows that if these beautiful, God-given passions are twisted to feed self, then they will destroy not only the man but also his family. Let's take a look at how this is happening today.

At twelve billion dollars a year in the U.S., the revenues of the pornography industry are bigger than the NFL, NBA, and Major League Baseball combined. Three billion of this revenue is generated by illegal child pornography alone. Worldwide porn sales are reported to be fifty-seven billion dollars. To put this in perspective, the combined revenues of ABC, CBS, and NBC are $6.2 billion.[4]

---

4. Jerry Ropelato, "Internet Pornography Statistics," http://internet-filter-review.toptenreviews.com/internet-pornography-statistics.html, Nov. 19, 2006.

It seems that the whole of our society has been designed by the enemy of our souls to destroy men, to keep them from becoming what God designs they should be; for if real men stand at the head of families, the devil loses the freedom to attack and deceive the family members. No wonder men find temptation to impurity everywhere we look in this world. It calls for your attention from the billboards as you drive into town. It grabs your eyes as you wait in the checkout line at the grocery store. It saturates the music that throbs from our radios and stereos. It parades itself on the magazine racks, in the general television programming, and throughout most of the available movies. The fashion industry persuades women to dress in ways that accentuate their sensuality. Everywhere a man turns is the not-so-subtle message "A man has sexual needs. He deserves to have those needs met. Satisfy them now. If it feels good, then do it." Then he is offered a variety of ways to do just that: masturbation, pre-marital and extra-marital affairs, prostitution, homosexuality, pornography (both on and off the Internet), and child molestation.

Even the marriage bed itself is perverted. Many men think that if they are married, they can do whatever they want with their wives and it is OK. But that's just not true.[5] Lust is just as destructive within marriage as outside of it. For instance, Macho Joe asserted, "I don't really think I have a problem with sexual addiction. I don't go to prostitutes. I'm not interested in having an affair and would never molest a child. Twice a day is enough for me!" When questioned as to what he meant by "twice a day," he indicated that he was having sex with his wife twice every day! If she resisted, he would use physical restraint to the point of making her nothing more than a puppet. Joe was not being intimate with his wife. Instead, he was using her as an object to masturbate with while fantasizing about other women. The sexual perversions devised by the devil—even in the marriage bed—are limitless in quantity and in destructiveness.

If you are fortunate enough to have been spared these ravages of the devil, praise God and your parents for their protective care. You probably don't need this information. Please feel free to skip the rest of this chapter.

---

5. See Hebrews 13:4.

JAIL CELLS

But while these are not pleasant subjects to deal with, for the overwhelming majority of men, at least one item on this list is a major concern that robs them of peace with God and hinders their Christian growth. These temptations affect men in every walk of life and economic situation. Many who struggle in these areas are nice, sincere people and, not uncommonly, respected leaders in their churches and communities. Because these subjects are not openly talked about, most of us have come to believe that we are the only ones struggling in these areas. When we are too afraid to confess our need and our sin, we remain isolated and locked within our jail cell.

Let's briefly examine some of these jail cells and then let's move on to the solution—the God who came to set the captives free!

In *The Sexual Man*,[6] Dr. Archibald Hart surveyed some six hundred Christian men on the subject of masturbation. Of the married men who responded, 61 percent said they masturbated, with 82 percent of those saying they did it at least once a week. Ninety-six percent of single men under the age of twenty admitted to a masturbation habit.

Since so many Christian men are making love to themselves, it seems logical that they must find it satisfying, right? Wrong. Dr. Hart's survey showed that only 23 percent gave "enjoyment" as their reason for doing it. The rest said "habit," "their sex drive," they "were addicted to it," or "lack of an outlet for sex" as the reason they engaged in masturbation.

The problem is that sex is about connecting and communicating spirit to spirit with our wife. When a man masturbates, there is no other person to connect with, so an emotional misfire takes place. Instead of bonding with another in warmth, intimacy, and love, they end up being haunted by loneliness, isolation, and shame. These painful emotions call for relief, and the vicious cycle is perpetuated.

---

6. Archibald Hart, *The Sexual Man* (Nashville: W Publishing Group, 1999).

Let me illustrate with this testimony from my friend Ray:

> I grew up an only child with parents who were unable to
> bond with me in a way that provided the warmth and love that
> I needed, and I was often left home alone. It was in my loneli-
> ness and isolation that I began to fantasize about girls. Then I
> discovered masturbation and the temporary comfort it brought.
> For a time, it was enjoyable and it helped to mask the pain of
> my loneliness. But the pain did not go away. In fact, the pain
> intensified as the guilt and shame of my impure thoughts and
> actions increased. This brought the felt need for more. I turned
> to pornography and to 'acting out' in some very destructive
> ways. But it was never enough. I was out of control of my life
> and I felt worthless.

ONE THING LEADS TO ANOTHER

Ray needed love, not lust. The devil tricked him into using a counterfeit that only made things worse, not better. He discovered that lust
is a tyrant—always demanding more. Those who give in to masturbation find impure thoughts pressuring them. Fantasy life opens the door
to a number of temptations because what is exciting one day becomes
commonplace the next. Boredom promotes the need for new images or
ideas, and pornography is often the next logical step. The man flatters
himself that since no other party is involved, there is nothing wrong
with his thought life.

Jesus does not agree. He stated in no uncertain terms that "whosoever looketh on a woman to lust after her hath committed adultery with
her already in his heart."[7] We shouldn't be fooled. These lustful fantasies are not harmless. They are destructive in a number of ways. First, no
woman is capable of living up to the fantasies conjured up in the mind
of an impure man. By indulging in these thought patterns, men set
themselves up not only to be disappointed with their wives but also to
relate to their wives in ways God never intended. The very woman God

---

7. Matthew 5:28.

has provided to be your companion becomes boring and unattractive as your mind compares her with the women in your fantasies. Marital discord and unhappiness become a sure reality.

Ray's testimony continues:

> In my late teens, I came to believe that getting married would fix my problem and that I would never have trouble with my sexual issues again, but I was sadly mistaken. It only seemed to help for the first few weeks. After the newness of the marriage began to wear off, I was right back to my fantasies and masturbation. I was emotionally unable to bond with my wife, because of my unreal expectations and because of my lack of bonding to my parents and my siblings (since I had no siblings). I couldn't be honest with my wife because I had so much to hide. I discovered that, without honesty in my marriage, there could be no real intimacy. And, without true intimacy, I was pushed deeper into my addiction.

As Ray discovered, the emotional baggage associated with this habit makes it impossible for some men to connect emotionally or physically with their wives, and they hide in their habits to avoid the risks of real relationship.

Other men are conditioned for physical adultery—almost in the way an athlete is trained. Athletes have learned that training mentally as well as physically opens the door to great achievement. For example, if you want to pole vault a certain height, you repeatedly imagine yourself doing so. You think about each detail and how it feels when you plant the pole and arch your body up and over the pole. You imagine the thrill and falling to the mat—after setting a new record. It sounds strange, but it really works and helps them do more than just physically preparing would. Now if I were the devil and I wanted you to engage in improper activities, I would want you to mentally imagine yourself engaged in such activity, over and over, as many times as possible, so that when the temptation presents itself to engage in the activity with a real person in real life, the mental pattern of behavior is already developed and, for some, it just seems to happen *naturally*.

For example, J. B. was a professed Christian and an elder in his church, but while sitting on the platform with the pastor, waiting for his part in the service, he was sizing up the women in the congregation, looking for his next conquest. In his mind, he would undress her and imagine himself having sex with her. Very often, he would later find himself actually in bed with one of the women he had fantasized about. His mental "exercise" prepared the way for carrying out his fantasies.

It's not all it's cracked up to be

There is always the temptation to fulfill our unmet desires outside the bounds of marriage. But unlike J. B., very few of the men I have counseled set out to have an "affair." Usually a relationship starts quite innocently and grows into something more than either party expected. Nevertheless, infidelity exacts a heavy toll on both the man and his other relationships. The Bible has some rather strong things to say that spell out the dangers. "But whoso committeth adultery with a woman lacketh understanding: he that doeth it destroyeth his own soul. A wound and dishonour shall he get; and his reproach shall not be wiped away."[8]

Few people find unfaithfulness all it is cracked up to be. More often than not, they find themselves burdened with guilt, shame, and remorse. In addition, if they do marry their new lover, they quickly find that they have simply added to the problems they face.

Disappointing dead ends

Then there is the Internet, which we have already mentioned. According to one survey, 60 percent of all Web site visits are sexual in nature, and as many as 80 percent of those visitors to sex sites were spending so much time tracking down erotica on the computer that they were putting their real-life relationships and/or jobs at risk.[9] The Internet's illusion of anonymity combined with easy access opens the door for explorations that might never take place in another setting.

---

8. Proverbs 6:32, 33.

9. MSNBC Survey 2000, quoted on AFO.net, Nov. 19, 2006, http://www.afo.net/statistics.htm.

"My addiction to pornography," J. B. testifies, "began many years before the Internet started. When I had to go to a store to get my porn, it was embarrassing and I had a lot of fear that someone I knew would see me. And, there was always the danger that my wife would find my 'dirty' magazines. That was somewhat of a deterrent. I didn't go there often. But, when the Internet came 'of age,' access to pornography became as easy as a couple of 'mouse' clicks on my computer while sitting in the privacy of my locked office."

Online chat has made it possible for us to interact with people the world over whom we might never have had opportunity to know before, but it also has a more sinister side, and that is cyber affairs—complete with online, virtual sex. Even more troubling is that many men believe such affairs are not cheating. They even rationalize that when they participate in cyber sex they are actually doing their wife a favor by not forcing them to have sex when they don't want it (like Joe did in an earlier illustration). However, as we mentioned before, God does not agree. He said "whosoever looketh on a woman to lust after her hath committed adultery with her already in his heart."[10]

I wish there was no need to mention prostitution, but there is. Every young man and woman should grow up understanding the plight of people who have no skills and nothing to offer except their own body. Many are forced into the business, some in virtual slavery, and no Christian man should participate in this dark industry in any form. J. B. admits, "When I didn't have an active affair going on and the porn got boring, I would sometimes sink so low as to go to a prostitute. The emotional comfort of this act would only last as long as the orgasm because I could see the pain in her face. My guilt and shame was immense. I only went to a prostitute when I was at my worst."

Then, there are "girlie shows" and "nudie" bars. I know of situations at Christian colleges where the guys head out at night to such locations to drink and watch naked women. Not only are such actions not edifying, they are downright dangerous to your future happiness because they present a warped picture of women to young men who are soon going to be forming their own marriages. The

---

10. Matthew 5:28.

women in such an environment appear totally sexual and at your service (so they can get your money, of course), and no woman you marry is going to live up to the false image of sexuality presented. Hence, the stage is set for unrealistic expectations and crushing disappointment on every side in the marriage. Consider these words of Solomon: "For the lips of a strange woman drop as an honeycomb, and her mouth is smoother than oil: But her end is bitter as wormwood, sharp as a twoedged sword. Her feet go down to death; her steps take hold on hell."[11]

Perhaps the sickest of all the perversions is child molestation. Perpetrators often target children rather than adults because they are easier to woo and control. Children are powerless individuals, dependent on the adults in their lives to provide safety and sustenance. Their minds do not have the maturity to handle the implications of sexual intimacy. It is not love to them—it is trauma. Often they are incapable of asking for help, and when they do, they are sometimes not believed, or worse yet, they are blamed for seducing the perpetrator. They feel guilty, dirty, exploited, and fearful.

In other cases, a child may be wooed with what appears to be love by a relative, teacher, or family friend. The naïve child is brainwashed to believe that being sexual with this person is good, healthy, and maybe even necessary. They may not recognize this behavior as abuse until many years later, but their lack of understanding does not preclude the damage inflicted.

It is one of the greatest of betrayals for a trusted adult to prostitute a child for his own unmet needs. The implications for that child are lifelong and not easily healed. God has compassion for both victim and perpetrator because often the perpetrator has been a victim himself, but He also said that it would be better for that man to have a huge boulder tied to his neck and be dropped into the ocean than to live out that kind of exploitation.[12] We must do all in our power as men to stop or prevent this kind of abuse and to heal both the cause and the result of the sickness.

---

11. Proverbs 5:3–5.
12. See Matthew 18:6; Mark 9:42; Luke 17:2.

Healing the sickness

There is a story I'll call an urban legend about some movers who were relocating a minister. A number of parishioners had gathered to help load the truck, and as they carried a heavily loaded box out of the house, the bottom gave way, spilling the minister's pornography collection all over the ground in front of the astonished onlookers. The minister frantically dropped down to his knees to gather up the offensive items, and one of the members was heard to state, "It looks like that's the longest you've spent on your knees in quite some time, Pastor."

This poor pastor, humiliated though he was, is no worse or better than any of the other men standing there. He is a sinner in need of repentance, forgiveness, and restoration just like the rest of us. Attitudes of disdain toward individuals because of their specific areas of weakness ignore the basic facts of Christ's whole ministry. Jesus, our Example, reached out, redeemed, and honored with His presence and friendship the very ones society refused—the demoniac, the leper, the harlot.

No one else on earth may know what goes on in your private life, and certainly no one can read your thoughts. Most of us are grateful for this because deep down we fear that if people knew what we were, they wouldn't want to have anything to do with us. But God knows exactly what goes on. Not one thought, look, or action is hidden from Him. He sees our depravity, feels our misery, and knows the strength of our temptation. He knows how powerless we are to change on our own, and yet He does not despise us. The more desperate and helpless and ashamed we find ourselves, the more God knows we need Him. He longs to embrace us and provide us with what we really need—genuine relationship. He has a solution for every crisis, every problem, and every temptation. Let's explore together Jesus' steps to freedom.

Step 1: Honesty

Remember when Ray said, "I was out of control of my life and I felt worthless"? He may not have realized it at the time, but he was entering into his first step to freedom—honesty. It's a hard step to take. It seems easier to deny it, to excuse it, to blame others for it, to do anything to avoid facing it.

But you cannot find freedom while avoiding that first step, honestly taking responsibility for your own character—what you think, how you feel, and how you behave. While circumstances might affect you, you are the only one who can decide how you will respond. As long as you blame someone or something else, you will remain a victim of your own lust. You need to evaluate just where the current direction of your life is taking you. Do you really want to destroy yourself, your loved ones, and your hope of heaven?[13]

I encourage you to be honest about who you really are and who you really are not—with yourself, with God, and with at least one other safe person. The Bible exhorts us to confess our faults to one another and to pray for each other, because the intensely earnest prayer of a Christian is worth a lot in God's economy.[14] You may fear the vulnerability such honesty entails, but it is the safest, wisest thing to do. By making ourselves accountable to God and trusted friends, we accelerate our healing process.

Most of us have formed our opinion of what God is like based on what our parents and church members are like. Because of this, we often have misunderstandings about God. There are many people—even Christians—who do not trust God. For many, like Ray, it has been helpful to make a disconnection between God and those people who have wrongly represented God's character.

My God is so full of love that even if you were the only sinner in the world, He would still have come down, lived as a man, and died for your sins. You can trust my God. He will never lead you in any way that you would not choose to be led if you could see the future yourself.

So, open your heart wide to Him. Surrender those ugly things that bring you so much pain. It will feel like you are cutting off your right arm or gouging out your right eye,[15] but when you finally stop pretending, blaming, or excusing, you will find that God's big arms of love are there to embrace you just as you are. You will no longer be alone with

---

13. See Ephesians 5:3–6; Colossians 3:5, 6; Hebrews 12:14; Revelation 21:7, 8.
14. See James 5:16.
15. See Matthew 5:29, 30.

your problem—God is there for you. He is able to do far more for you than you can even imagine.[16] He is your divine Coach—especially where you are weakest[17]—and He is capable of guiding you to the winning play in every match.[18]

Step 2: A clean heart

Many have the idea that once they confess and repent of their sin, they must then grit their teeth and just not do it anymore. But God is not satisfied to see us merely abstaining from the activities that are wrong. In fact, He knows this is a dead-end solution.[19] If we are only stuffing down our lustful thoughts and feelings, they will sooner or later erupt in outward actions. Besides that, it is a miserable existence, and God wants us to have abundant life![20]

He offers something far better. He is able and willing to cleanse the heart and free us from within. He can change us to love purity and hate lust. We simply need to go to Him with the request that David prayed after his affair with Bathsheba: "Create in me a clean heart, O God; and renew a right spirit within me."[21] God responds, "Then I will sprinkle clean water upon you, and ye shall be clean: from all your filthiness, and from all your idols, will I cleanse you. A new heart also will I give you, and a new spirit will I put within you: and I will take away the stony heart out of your flesh, and I will give you an heart of flesh. And I will put my spirit within you."[22]

He will fill our empty fuel tanks with Him. Freedom is found when an empty, starved, miserable heart is filled with the love of God. If a man abstains from sin but still has an empty heart, in the end he will go back to lust or some other counterfeit love. What we're really after is to have our heart filled with something much more powerful, more wonderful, and purer than lust. Once we've tasted and known the inner

---

16. See Ephesians 3:20.
17. See 2 Corinthians 12:9.
18. See Jude 1:24.
19. See James 1:14, 15; Matthew 12:34.
20. See John 10:10.
21. Psalm 51:10.
22. Ezekiel 36:25–27.

sweetness of the very God Himself in the core and center of our hearts, we gain the power to live up to His standard of sexual purity. A heart that's thriving and responding with the love of God has no hunger for the pathetic counterfeits like lust. When we make knowing and loving God our goal, we gain sexual purity. But when we make mere abstinence the goal, we'll continue to fail, because there's no power in merely gritting our teeth.

STEP 3: DON'T MAKE PROVISION FOR YOUR FLESH

When God gives us a new heart, it is still our responsibility to make no provision for the flesh. We must run from sexual immorality. Job set a good example for us when he said, " 'I made a solemn pact with myself never to undress a girl with my eyes.' "[23]

Go into a huddle with your divine Coach and evaluate what triggers temptation for you. With Jesus, form a plan of action—a fire escape—an actual step-by-step plan of behavior so that you will not fall when you are tempted and do all you humanly can to prepare the way for your salvation. If fatigue makes you vulnerable, change your schedule and activities to combat the fatigue. If being alone sets you off, cultivate appropriate relationships. If driving to work takes you by billboards that trigger impure thoughts, take a different route or plan with God what you can do to replace the impure thoughts with good ones. Listen to pure, uplifting music; put on an inspiring CD; memorize and meditate on Scripture. You cannot afford to give the wrong thoughts a moment's notice. If you do, your emotions will get riled up, and it will be much harder to recover yourself than if you never started down that path.

If you find yourself caught up in a situation that you know in your heart of hearts is wrong, then in the strength of Christ break it off. If you have been involved with someone at work, break it off and transfer to a different branch of the company or take a different job, but don't place yourself in a place of temptation. It is better for a family to move to a new location than to leave one of its members in a place of moral danger.

---

23. Job 31:1, *The Message*.

If the Internet poses temptation for you, get help with filters, special Internet providers, or accountability software. If this is not sufficient deterrent, then cut off your Internet access.

Find a Christian brother who will neither condemn you for your weakness nor coddle you in it. A friend who will pray for you and encourage you through the difficult time of temptation—as well as hold you accountable—can be a great help in this battle.

Physical fitness plays a big part in the struggle. A healthy, strong body lends well to a healthy strong mind and spirit. Eating a wholesome, well-balanced diet and engaging regularly in a vigorous exercise program can go a long way toward helping you make good decisions when temptation to lust raises its ugly head.

STEP 4: CHANGE CHANNELS

One of the most effective tools to guarantee victory is changing channels. Let me show you how it works.

I had counseled with Pete a number of times about marriage. His wife is one of those people who feels loved when she receives words of affection, while Pete desires the tender touches of love. The problem was that this was Pete's third marriage, and he had some long-standing habits. His early life had taught him to try to satisfy his own needs through lust. Before he married Sharon, he had given up masturbation as the means to do this, but unfortunately, he had slipped into the sad and almost unconscious belief that his wife was to be the vehicle that replaced that habit. Therefore, when his wife did anything that displeased him, something all of us do inadvertently to our spouse on occasion, he would become sullen and cold. In place of the loving affirmation his wife desired, she received harsh, cutting words. When he didn't get his way, he excluded his spouse from his affections, in effect sending her to her own emotional corner as if she was his opponent rather than his wife.

She was understandably hurt by his actions and yet, come evening, he expected her to perform wonderfully and passionately. Finally she said, "No! Either learn to love me throughout the day or expect no lovemaking at night."

Yet he still couldn't seem to break out of his long established habits. In spite of his actions, he blamed her for all their marriage problems, demeaning her frigidity and inability to perform. He continued to treat her coldly and, of course, there was no intimacy between them. Pete was miserable, and so was his wife, but the ball was in his court and he refused to put forth the effort to cooperate with God so that he could be changed inside. You see, unless we change the inside—our thoughts, our attitudes, and our concepts—our outward actions will not change. A lot of us are like Pete. We may have some problem, but we simply grit our teeth and endure rather than cooperating with our divine Coach for a better strategy.

Pete and I talked about all these things, but I don't think they sank in because six to nine months later, he called me with a real "pity party" attitude. He wanted to tell me all the ways she'd done him wrong, but I cut it off as soon as I could. "Pete, you remind me of a man who comes home, gets a big bowl of popcorn and his favorite drink, then puts his feet up watching his usual channel all the while complaining continually about what's on. Not just once mind you, but night after night after night—one pity party after another, unhappy with the way things are, but never altering his behavior. Pete, you need to change channels!"

"What do you mean?"

Flip to another program

"Just what I said. Grab hold of your remote and change the channel. When you are tempted to sit down in front of 'the things I don't like in my wife' program, change the channel! Change to the channel of reminiscing over all your good times, or the channel replaying your wedding or honeymoon. Maybe flip to the courtship program and review in your mind all the things you liked about Sharon."

"Jim, I'm afraid that wouldn't be very easy. These days I can't seem to find much positive about her."

"Of course, it won't be easy. It is impossible to do in your own strength, but it is very possible when you invite God into your thoughts and emotions. Ask Him to take away your pity party feelings and replace them with a praise party, extolling all the great attributes of your wife. Sure you have an old established habit to overcome and you're likely to find you've flipped back to the old channel without much thought, but as soon as you realize it, change it back. You are changing habits from looking at the negative to focusing on her happiness, lightening her burdens. It may seem contrived at first, but rehearse in your mind honest, heart-felt, affirming words. Practice saying them out loud to her. Soon they will actually be expressing the feelings of your heart as you share them. Stay on this channel of admiring and cherishing her."

You may have to fight this battle every few minutes or even every few moments, until new habits are established. In so doing, you are following the admonition of Scripture to think on "good" things.[24]

This may be a terrible struggle—perhaps the greatest battle you have ever fought, but it will lead to the life free from the tyranny of your selfish emotions and thoughts. It is one thing to accept salvation from Christ, but it is quite another to enter into salvation by working with Christ to correct patterns of wrong thoughts and actions.

TRY IT . . . IT WORKS!

Prepare in advance to find a new channel so you can get to it in a hurry when you have a relapse. This becomes a faith that works, and it works very practically in our lives. Daily practice will make this experience yours, and with time these healthy new habits will become stronger than your old destructive habits. It works not only in marriage issues but also on virtually any taboo subject you may be struggling with. I have seen it win over masturbation, premarital sex, pornography, prostitution, immoral thoughts, homosexuality, and a whole host of other temptations that the followers of Christ struggle with.

When sexual desire hits, go to God. Surrender yourself to Him. Give Him your thoughts and emotions and ask Him to help you replace them with new thoughts and emotions. Enter into your "fire escape." Think on the beautiful things of life. Change channels, and a life of freedom and liberty will be yours. You may be thinking that you are not strong enough to enter into this kind of surrender. But God has promised that no matter how weak you are,[25] and no matter how strong the temptation is, He will provide a way of escape.[26] He is our Coach! He

---

24. Philippians 4:8.
25. See 2 Corinthians 12:9.
26. See 1 Corinthians 10:13.

always has a winning play! Cooperate with Him. Choose to take His way of escape in that moment of decision.

If you stumble and fall, learn from your mistakes and move on. Failure is a teacher; learn from it, make adjustments, and keep advancing until you have a new habit and a new you.

My friend Ray applied these four principles and found lasting freedom. He shares the following thoughts:

> For many years now, I have been in recovery from my life of disgusting sexual perversions. After I realized my own powerlessness over my addictions and came to believe that God— a power greater than myself—could restore my sanity, I began to learn about and to practice these principles of surrender that you teach. Each time a temptation would come, I would totally surrender myself to God, realizing my helplessness and His all-powerfulness, praying—like Paul did when he was struck down with the glory of Jesus—" 'Lord, what do You want me to do?' "[27] I can testify to you today that every time I have cooperated with divine agencies in this way, God has turned my powerlessness into victory! Without fail, He has delivered—and continues to deliver—me from temptation. This is how (I believe) God is creating within me a new heart.[28] Each time I surrender in this way, my faith is strengthened, my heart toward God is softened, and more and more those things that I once loved, I begin to hate. And, the principles of God's kingdom become more and more desirable. I praise God for recovery!

One of the hardest, most seemingly impossible, cases I ever worked with was a gay couple that wanted to break from their former ways. Let me tell you, they were facing an uphill battle against heavily ingrained patterns of thought that had ruled them for many, many years. I shared about changing channels, and they both entered in. Success was achieved

---

27. Acts 9:6, NKJV.
28. See Ezekiel 36:26.

over cultivated behaviors. For a long time they worked together to achieve a new and better life. However, after a while, one tired of the protracted effort and went back to his former lifestyle, leaving both his faith and his partner behind. The other persevered, and today he lives a life that honors God.

Devil's Ploys Drive Me to Freedom?

I have practiced this habit of changing channels for many years and find the devil's ploys are driving me ever closer to Sally—my queen and the love of my life. Here's how it works. When I see a billboard or a magazine cover portraying improperly dressed or seductively posed women, I have learned to change channels and look away, replacing those impure images the devil threw in front of me with other thoughts:

I love Sally!

She's the prettiest little thing I've ever set eyes on!

She satisfies all *my desires! No one could be better.*

She is s-o-o-o thoughtful and s-o-o-o helpful.

I love her smile, her sweet little laugh, her playfulness, her doting over me.

Why, I could never find any one better for me.

In fact, I'm going over to the florist to buy her some flowers.

If the florist is closed, I saw some daisies back there beside the road. I think I'll pick her a bouquet of those!

I'm going to call her right now and woo her because she is my gal—my Sal.

Oh Lord, increase my love for the only *girl of my life. Lord, help me to love her more, think of her more often; remind me of all the little things I can do to win her heart.*

I think you get the picture. A truth often repeated is finally believed. A life of faith is not a *passive* one of mentally accepting Christ as your Savior. No, it is an *active* one of God initiating through my conscience and my will following through. You can see that if I am faithful to change channels, I am actively cooperating with God. The devil will throw more temptations in my path, and the more I cooperate with God, the more I fall in love with my Sally.

Go ahead—try it out! Everyone who's tried it tells me it works—if they work at it! It's been working for Ray, J. B., and many others for years now. You too can work it, because you are worth it! So kill the taboos in your life and experience the freedom God designed you to have. As you cooperate with God, you will live above the pull of your flesh. You will be an *empowered* man!

CHAPTER 12

━━━━━ TOUCHING THE TABOO ━━━━━

Questions to Consider for Personal Inventory or Group Discussion

1. Have I bought into the devil's counterfeit for love—lust?
2. Do I view my sexual drive as a need that must be satisfied?
3. Do I abuse myself or sacrifice my wife or children on the altar of lust?
4. Do my sexual practices rob me of peace and leave me feeling ashamed?
5. Do I feel the need to hide what really goes on in my heart from my wife?
6. Am I rationalizing or excusing my behavior?
7. Do I feel alone and worthless? Do I fear being found out?
8. Are my thoughts pure? Would I be ashamed if others knew what I love to think about?
9. Am I being truly honest with myself, with God, and with at least one other trusted person about what I am facing in this area?
10. Am I willing to take the steps to freedom?
11. Do I know how to change channels and, if so, do I?
12. Have I prepared a "fire exit" for when I am tempted?

Jumbled Priorities

Lord, what wilt thou have me to do?
—Acts 9:6

"Dad, can we play kickball tonight? Please, can we?" twelve-year-old Jared begged as his father climbed out of his car after a day at the office.

"No, Son, I've got work to do tonight," Father replied, picking up his briefcase and heading for the back door of the house.

"What about tomorrow night, Father?" Jared pursued as he bounced his ball along behind his father.

"Sorry, Son, I have a church board meeting to attend."

"Well, what about Thursday night?" Jared wasn't giving up. His eyes pleaded with his father, but his father didn't notice as he hung up his coat.

"I promised to help Bill with his building project." Irritation tinged the tone of his voice.

"Maybe this weekend then. Could we? Could we?"

Father was plainly peeved now. "Just leave me alone, Son. You know I'm busy!"

Jared turned away, tears stinging his eyes. *Maybe those older boys next door will have time for me,* he thought.

HOPSCOTCH AND HURRICANES

Another father relaxed in his recliner with the cordless phone as he discussed the latest church board meeting with the pastor. Seven-year-old Jenny dashed in the back door, letting it slam behind her. She ran up to Father, eagerness plainly written all over her. "Daddy, can you come out and play hopscotch with us?"

"Shhhh! Shhhh!" Hand over the receiver, he says to her, "I'm on the phone. Quiet! Go out and play with your little brother, Tony."

"But Daddy—"

"Later, later!"

Jenny's shoulders slump, and she walks slowly out the back door, disappointed.

Then later becomes today. Jenny and Tony approach Father at the breakfast table. "Daddy, can you help Tony and me build a fort in the woods?" Jenny ventures timidly.

"Not this week, sweetheart—I'm too busy," he replies between bites of toast as he scans the weather forecast on the nearby TV.

"Well, how about this weekend, Daddy?"

"No, I can't. Too much to do. Wow—look at the damage that hurricane has done," he comments to his wife as she joins them at the table.

"How about next week?" Jenny pressed.

"What? Oh, the fort. Well, maybe . . . maybe. Ask me then."

Jenny and Tony look at each other sadly. Dad doesn't notice because he is too busy flipping through the morning paper as he inhales his breakfast.

Jumbled priorities! I see this played out everywhere I go. "Dad has no time for me. He's too busy." But our children are not the only ones who long for a bit of time with us.

Just Waiting

Barbara is a lovely woman who has waited all day to talk with her husband, Bob, about something that troubles her. She is delighted when she sees his car pull into the driveway and meets him on the porch with an affectionate kiss and simple request. "Can we go for a walk after dinner—just the two of us—and talk?"

"Sure, honey. I'd love to."

Barbara's heart sings as she serves her family the lovely meal she has prepared. Just a little uninterrupted time with Bob will help a whole lot.

She can hardly wait! Then the phone rings. Suddenly, she is quite aware of the conversation as Bob says, "Yeah, Ralph, I'm almost done eating. Why don't you come right over, I've got plenty of time for you." Barbara's heart just sinks, and when Bob comes to bed much later, he wonders why she seems so cold.

GIRL TALK

My wife and I were invited to present a weekend seminar near a private Christian college. The girl's dean called to tell us she was bringing thirty-five of her girls to the meetings, and they wanted to talk privately with my wife, Sally. My wife agreed, and the girls came to the weekend meetings. When the time came for their meeting with Sally, however, I got a real surprise. All the girls talked and voted me in on the meeting!

What an opportunity! To hear what these young ladies really thought! I was excited because I have no girls of my own. But my excitement soon turned to real concern.

"Mr. Hohnberger, how do I know which guy is the right one for me?" Amy asked.

"Well, Amy, first you must consider his spiritual condition. Does he love God and order his life after godly principles? Is your time together spiritually uplifting? Are you compatible in the major areas of lifestyle, recreation, and future goals? On the practical side, has he shown the potential to support himself and a prospective family? Is there a natural spark of attraction between you? Is each of you adaptable, able to blend your lives into one? Can you see God's hand clearly leading in your relationship? And last of all, while this is your decision, there is much wisdom in seeking the counsel of those who know you best, especially your parents."

I could see her countenance fall as she studied the floor.

"What's the matter, Amy?" I inquired gently.

"I can't talk to my parents like that."

"Why not? Haven't they talked with you your whole life about your friends—the things you like about them and the things you don't?"

I didn't expect tears, but that is what I suddenly got. I worried she might have tragically lost her parents, but she continued through her tears. "My parents were always too busy for me."

Another girl rose to her feet. "Can I bring my young man to your home, for you to evaluate?"

"Why don't you ask your own father?"

"Oh, he's too busy. He's a pastor with two churches."

TUG OF WAR

Jumbled priorities! We all experience it. Most of us find life to be a constant chase after unfinished tasks and upset people while those who need us most have to wait. We live in a perpetual tug of war between the urgent hassles of day-to-day living and the essential matters of life—between the press of the moment that *demands* our immediate attention and that which is truly meaningful and important. Our lives are ordered by the dictates of society, by the constraints of our occupation, by the expectations of others. Most of the time, the press of the moment wins.

We inevitably reap the unfailing result of jumbled priorities: stressed-out bodies, fractured relationships, and superficial spirituality. We desperately need relief!

Perhaps God was wrong. If He knew we couldn't get it all done in twenty-four hours, should He have made the day thirty hours long instead? Mercy, Lord! A longer day wouldn't solve our problems. We just like to think it would. "Next year," we tell ourselves, "next year I'll have more time!" Come on. Who are we kidding? All of us know by now that the rush is constant, the press is ever present, and the demands of life are never ending. I can't tell you the number of people I have met over the years who have bought into the idea that they will escape the stresses they are under just as soon as they clear up this or that temporary crisis. When I meet them one, two, three, or even five years later, they are still in that same tug of war.

PRESSURE COOKER

Because we have lived so long in this rushed and stressed-out condition, we begin to think of it as normal. We even think it is normal to live this way at home. We forget that our homes were designed by God to be little sanctuaries from the stresses of the world. Instead, the very things they were intended to shut out have invaded them. We find ourselves living in a pressure cooker.

For one thing, the telephone interrupts our every waking moment. It interrupts our meals, it interrupts our conversations with our families, and it interrupts our quiet time with God. And then, to top it off, we have call waiting so that even our interruptions can be interrupted. I protest! Call waiting is not based upon heavenly principle. Let me explain: When I am talking with God, He gives me His undivided attention as if there were not another person on earth, and He does the same for all the others who pray to Him at the same time. Don't ask me how He does it, but I know He does. He doesn't say, "Hang on a minute, Jim. I've got another call coming in from Bradley." If God put me on hold, it would really irk me.

A friend asked me to go on a backcountry climbing trip just over the Canadian border. Now I love the wilderness, and it didn't take much arm-twisting to get me to agree. However, as we were nearing the summit of Starvation Peak, feasting our eyes on the spectacular panorama of giant peaks and jeweled lakes, listening to the shrill call of the red-tailed hawk, and inhaling the clean air, a strange noise intruded. What was that? Certainly not a sound from the wilderness! My friend quickly reached into his backpack for his satellite phone and began carrying on a business deal.

"Will you turn that thing off?" I half asked and half demanded. "We're in the wilderness. That thing doesn't belong here!"

You see, I go to the wilderness to come close to my God. As I hike among the mighty mountains, I gain a sense of my puniness, my own weakness, and my tremendous need for God. But all this can be stolen away when we use this setting as just another place to conduct our business.

It is focus and priority that determine what we take with us from a trip such as the one above. One person can come and meet with God and go away changed, and another can enjoy the view, the company, even the meals cooked in the coals of a fire, and take nothing of lasting spiritual significance with them. The same is true of our home life. It can be a sanctuary, or we can allow all sorts of intrusions like the telephone to desecrate it.

We found that we had to take control of our phone or it would control us! How did we do it? We learned to screen our calls and to set aside certain times of the day when we don't answer the phone—never during meals, worship, family time, or (when the boys were home-schooling) during study hours.

Thief in the Living Room

Perhaps no home invader has done more to promote the misuse of our time, the perversion of our passions, and the moral breakdown of the family than the television. It was bad enough when only broadcast television existed, but now cable TV and satellite TV bring more choices and more evil into our homes than ever before. It is a powerful medium that strongly influences our thinking, behavior, and use of time.

In the average American home, the television is viewed almost eight hours a day.[1] Over two decades ago I decided to get rid of it, and our family replaced evening TV time with family time—every evening at six-thirty. As we tasted the joys of family fun and family talk time, we found we had no desire for television. It is a poor substitute for family companionship!

Another substitute many fall for is video mania. We think we must have something to entertain us. But just a momentary mental comparison of DVD jacket covers with Philippians 4:8[2] tells you that the vast majority of DVDs will not only occupy your time but will also dumb down your mind, reshape your focus, and destroy the fabric of your family values.

Videos are not evil in and of themselves, and they do allow a greater measure of control than the TV. But we must remember that every minute spent watching them is a minute not spent in positive interaction with our loved ones while, perhaps, at the same time, training them to desire a poor substitute for us. This doesn't necessarily mean we should eliminate videos; however, it does mean we should allow God to lead, evaluating its effect on our families and then altering our usage accordingly.

---

1. *Newsweek,* Oct. 3, 2005, p. 62.

2. "Finally, brethren, whatsoever things are true, whatsoever things are honest, whatsoever things are just, whatsoever things are pure, whatsoever things are lovely, whatsoever things are of good report; if there be any virtue, and if there be any praise, think on these things."

Sally and I—with our two boys gone now—generally set aside one evening every other week as our "date night" when we plan to watch a DVD together. We choose only DVDs that are spiritually uplifting, that illustrate principle and true purpose. Sally might pop some popcorn and we snuggle up together to watch our selection. When it is finished, we talk about it: What was valuable and what was not? How does it relate to our life? We use it as a tool to deepen our understanding of each other and our perspective on life.

DISTRACTING

Then there are computers and the Internet. I have met many men who are more devoted to their computers than they are to their wives. They know the Internet better than they know their own children. They spend more time surfing the Web than listening to their divine Coach. This has become one more avenue for the devil to bring the bombardment of the world right into our homes.

To find the proper balance, we must ask ourselves why we spend time with the computer. Is it a tool to do necessary work? Or is it a diversion from a deeper call? Limiting our computer use to the essentials only can free significant time for the real priorities in life.

A WAY OUT?

The bottom line to the solution for jumbled priorities is more than screening our phone calls and limiting our entertainment. It's found in the example of Jesus. He, too, had to battle between the urgent and the essential. In fact, if any man was ever involved in a colossal tug of war, Jesus was! As I studied His life, I found the deeper answer I was looking for.

The first thing I noticed about Jesus was that *He knew the work His Father called Him to in the present.* He constantly breathed the prayer, "Lord, what wilt thou have me to do?"[3]—now, this moment, today? Don't miss this point. It is crucial! Jesus didn't look around to see what work *needed* to be done or *could* be done or that He was *qualified* to do. Instead, He constantly inquired of His Father, "What wilt thou have me to do *at this time?*"

3. Acts 9:6.

For example, as Jesus was teaching one day, an urgent message came to Him. "Now a certain man was sick, named Lazarus, of Bethany, the town of Mary and her sister Martha. (It was that Mary which anointed the Lord with ointment, and wiped his feet with her hair, whose brother Lazarus was sick.) Therefore the sisters sent unto him, saying, Lord, behold, he whom thou lovest is sick."[4]

Lazarus was dying, and Jesus had the power to heal him. Jesus' friends were so sure that He would drop what He was doing that they didn't even finish their request. Surely He would come right away! Do you feel the call? Can you identify with it? What would you have done? The need was absolute. The crisis was urgent. There were implicit demands—expectations, if you will, from those as close to Christ as any we know of.[5]

Jesus *only* followed His Father's will *in the present.* "When he heard therefore that he was sick, he *abode two days still* in the same place where he was."[6]

Christ didn't chase the urgent! Why not? The message about Lazarus's illness must have torn at His heart; for He knew such a message was not sent lightly. This is where you and I get in trouble. Our emotions tug at us, and we respond. Amid the crisis, however, Christ remained sensitive to God's will no matter how much it might have crossed His will or even His common sense and emotions.

That is the number-one key for us, too! It is recognizing the wisdom of our divine Coach and executing only those plays that He calls—not the ones that the bystanders call or even the ones we *feel* called to! He promises, "*I* will instruct *thee* and teach *thee* in the way which *thou* shalt go."[7] Our problem is that we are accustomed to managing ourselves—to running our own game. We have selective communication with God. We turn to Him only in a crisis. In the case of Lazarus, we would have felt no need to consult with God. Our friendship and our emotions would have made it obvious what we should do—and we would have gone right down and healed Lazarus. I did

---

4. John 11:1–3.
5. See John 11:5.
6. John 11:6, italics added.
7. Psalm 32:8, italics added.

things this way for years, and here at last as I studied Jesus, I was catching a vision of why some of my plays didn't go so well. We hold occasional huddles with our Coach and then generally play the game as we see it. We turn Him on and off like a radio. But Jesus held continuous communion with His Father.

Do we really want to get on top of our lives? Then we must learn to live in the present with Jesus! How do we do this? "And in the morning, rising up a great while before day, he went out, and departed into a solitary place, and there prayed."[8] I believe this was not an isolated experience, but a habit cultivated by our Lord. He renewed His connection with His Father every morning, and He never let go. Sometimes He got His instructions for the day while on His knees! However, often He received His directions in the moment as He communed with His Father throughout the day. That's why He could live above the tyranny of the urgent, the demands of others, and the rush and press of life. That's what enabled Him to stand solid as a rock amid the turbulent crowds and the deceptions of His enemies—at peace, serene in the knowledge that He was carrying out His Father's will.

We can taste of this experience if we are willing to enter into it. Many people tire of their devotional time with God because they are looking primarily for information rather than connection. Information alone is always incomplete. But connection with God supplies just what we need for each day. I have found through hard personal experience—and suspect you have as well—that listening to "self" as my coach destines me to miss the play. Still, I was doubtful I could find any happiness in letting God take control. I lingered for a time, hesitating. When I at last yielded to my Head Coach, I found—much to my astonishment—my life came into control.

BASE CAMP FIRST

The second key I noticed about Jesus was that He first learned how to add, then subtract, then multiply and divide. Jesus didn't go to phase 3 until phase 1 and 2 were in place. What I mean is that Jesus com-

---

8. Mark 1:35.

pleted being a child before He picked up the role of a youth and a man. He didn't rush into His ministry until each phase of His life was accomplished. Christ did not rush right out to convert the world the moment He realized His relationship to God as a youth. Nor did He when He turned eighteen or even when He turned twenty-one. He waited, doing what God willed Him to do at the time.

Toward the end of His earthly ministry, Jesus makes an incredible comment to His Father: " 'I have brought you glory on earth by completing the work you gave me to do.' "[9] I think there is more to this statement than just His years of active ministry. I believe that the three decades of quiet obscurity were just as much Jesus' work as His relatively few years of healing and teaching. When I realized that all my duties of the day could bring glory to God, be they mundane tasks or public evangelism, my attitude toward the mundane changed. I realized that God is a God of order and that He has a system to His training and work. We must enter into it at home before we are ready to take it to the world.

If we rush through phase 1 of the Christian life—which is making God our Head Coach—and phase 2—which is building up the home team—in order to reach a greater work, more fame, or larger acclaim; or to advance a cause or build a business, we find ourselves reaping the results of jumbled priorities.

NOT MY WILL

The third key: " 'For I have come down from heaven not to do my will but to do the will of him who sent me.' "[10] Christ was freed from the tyranny of the urgent because He fully embraced the will of His Father. You and I struggle more because we try to live a strange combination of self-direction and divine direction. However, Jesus could honestly say, " 'I always do what pleases him.' "[11] " 'I do nothing on my own.' "[12] The more we actively embrace God's will in place of our own, the greater freedom we will find from jumbled priorities.

---

9. John 17:4, NIV.
10. John 6:38, NIV.
11. John 8:29, NIV.
12. John 8:28, NIV.

So let's outline some very practical steps we can take to reorder our jumbled priorities in the strength of God.

STEP 1: DECIDE WHAT'S IMPORTANT[13]

Really, the issue we have to face is not the lack of time—everyone has the same number of hours in a day. Instead, the issue is what we do with our time! The world has predetermined this for us. It says that "things" are the number-one priority—a big home with nice furnishings, flashy cars, stylish fashions, a successful career with a big paycheck—you fill in the blank. The world says that "fun" is your number-one priority—whether that is sports, recreation, travel, a party life, or amusement parks. The world says to some that a life of ease is your number-one priority—no responsibility, being a couch potato while your wife or parents support you, or just getting along with the minimum. The world says to others that "fame and fortune" is your number-one priority—you must climb the ladder of corporate success, build your own business, or become a world-famous celebrity. The world, speaking through the church, even says that doing "a greater work" is your number-one priority—a ministry, outreach, or the "Lord's work." The world doesn't ask you. It just presses you into its mold and keeps you on its treadmill.

As Sally and I compared the world's dictates with Christ's life, we decided that our number-one priority would be relationships. When life is over, our things won't amount to much, our fun will have faded away, our easy street will hit a dead end, our fame and fortune will pass, and even our greater work will amount to nothing—if our relationships don't work.

So we sold our things; we changed our fun; we said Goodbye to fame and fortune; we found no time for a life of ease; and we realized we could not evangelize others if we hadn't evangelized our own marriage and our own boys.

We decided that instead of allowing the urgent to crowd out the essential, we would make time for the essential and let the urgent be crowded out if necessary. We found that a daily schedule was an

---

13. See Joshua 24:15.

essential tool to accomplish this, and we set certain things in concrete.

For instance, our highest priority was to find a life empowered by God.[14] So we set aside significant time in our day to study God's Word as it related to our practical lives and to connect with Him. We also set a time, morning and evening, to come together as a family to worship and talk about the Christian walk. We still follow this plan of life today and, with very few exceptions, do not allow this time to be stolen by the press of life.

We made our marriage number two on our priority list.[15] We gave time to each other daily. We scheduled talk time every afternoon from twelve-thirty to one o'clock, and we guarded that time. We made deliberate effort to cultivate the little attentions, little affections, and little sensitivities that mean so much to the other. We combined our efforts in building a marriage that really works, and under God we have one that is second to none. The spark of being in love has been recaptured and maintained for many years, and it isn't growing old but is more fun and exciting with each passing year.

Our third priority was our children.[16] We determined that somehow we were going to help them find the practical walk with God that we were finding. Once again, the daily schedule was an invaluable tool. We made ourselves available to them throughout the day and had meaningful interaction scheduled at family worship morning and evening, mealtimes, and family time every evening at six-thirty.

We didn't lose our boys to teenage rebellion as they got older. What we are recommending works in the real world. Both boys are now married with children of their own. In their own way, as suited for their own personalities, they are both adopting such a program in their own families, and we remain as close as ever.

Our fourth priority—making a living[17]—is related to the other points. Part of caring for our marriage and our children is providing for real physical needs while maintaining the balance of time needed for

---

14. See Matthew 6:33.
15. See Ephesians 5:33.
16. See Colossians 3:21.
17. See 1 Timothy 5:8.

God, the marriage, and the children. I didn't know how that could be done from our home in the wilderness, once our initial funds were exhausted, but God knew. And He provided a way for me to provide well for my family while keeping my priorities in balance. He's a good Coach!

Our fifth priority was reaching out to others. When you find something that works to unjumble your priorities and bring balance to your life, a spark to your marriage, and the hearts of your children to yours—you have something to share! And you want to share it! Share as God leads and opens the way while still maintaining proper balance!

STEP 2: SEE WHERE YOUR TIME IS ACTUALLY GOING

Once you've identified what's important to you, compare your priorities with where you actually spend your time. Keep a log for a few weeks, and you may find as I did that there is a definite tendency to neglect the essential for the urgent or, in the press of life, to forget it all together.

STEP 3: REDIRECT YOUR LIFE

Once you know where your time is going, redirect it to match your priorities. Don't wait for the world to give you permission to change. You must decide to act. To fail to decide is to decide. Start with a few changes—get on top of them, then institute more. Small successes motivate us to continue. Big failures set us up to throw in the towel. Many a man has tried to rebuild the world in a day and failed miserably. The journey is almost as important as the destination. Don't fret because it takes time to alter things—it will. Take one small step at a time. Don't be discouraged, but press on toward the mark of our high calling in Christ.

An important key to success here is to remember that when you add the best to your life, you must subtract something less valuable. If you don't, you will only end up feeling more pressured than ever.

STEP 4: FOLLOW THROUGH AND CONTINUALLY EVALUATE

I've known many to outline such a course on paper but never get around to putting it into practice. I've known others to start the process but lay it down feeling that it is too hard. Attitude is everything. Jesus' attitude was, "I can of mine own self do nothing."[18] But, "I can do all things through Christ which strengtheneth me."[19] Distractions will come in. Discouragements will present themselves. Others don't approve. Our wife doesn't follow through. We fail and think, *What's the use?*

When things break down, take courage![20] Even the best-trained army loses a battle. It's the war we want to win! Regroup, evaluate, and then press forward, remembering that God's "grace is sufficient for thee: for [His] strength is made perfect in weakness."[21]

CALLED OUT

The City of Stress in the Busy Valley of Distraction was a lonely place to live. In spite of the lively music, the party life, and the predictable rat race, the inhabitants were starving for genuine love, joy, and peace. One day they heard reports of a land high in the mountains free from stress and distraction. It was simply called The Peaceful Place.

A group of people decided to go and see it for themselves. Using SUVs and pick-ups to pull their heavily loaded trailers, they started out. As they traveled, the road began to ascend. On one side was a deep precipice while on the other side was a high rocky cliff. As they journeyed on, the road grew narrower and steeper to the point they concluded they could no longer travel safely with their trailers. Cramming as much of their luggage as they could into their vehicles, they left the trailers behind.

The road continued to narrow while it climbed until they could drive no farther. Loading their backpacks with what they could carry, they continued on foot. The narrow road became a slender path. They had to hug the rock wall to keep from falling down the steep precipice. As they did this, their backpacks pressed against the wall and caused them to sway toward the cliff. Fearing a fall, they unbuckled their packs and let them go.

18. John 5:30.
19. Philippians 4:13.
20. See Philippians 3:12, 14.
21. 2 Corinthians 12:9.

At this point, small cords were let down from the cliffs above, and they eagerly grasped them for balance, realizing thankfully that they were not alone. As they traveled, the cords moved along with them. The path finally became so narrow that they took off their hiking boots, and then a little later, their socks also.

They began to notice that at every change, some of their numbers were left behind. It was too much for some to give up their things and endure the hardships of the way. Those who persevered were only the more eager to get to the end.

Sounds from the Busy Valley of Distraction drifted up to them from time to time—the clamor of Wall Street bargaining, the thump of a rock band, the explosion of bombs in the Middle East, reports of rape and child molestation mingled with the canned laughter of a sit-com, the chorus of cheerleaders at the Super Bowl, political debates, and the lewd mockery of gay parades. The confusion of sound matched the hazy smog that obscured the depths.

Shuddering at the chaos below, the travelers pressed close to the rock wall yet could not place their feet fully upon the path, for it was too narrow. They then hung nearly their whole weight upon the cords, exclaiming: "We can do this! The cords are strong! They won't let us down!" Everyone repeated the encouragement to each other.

At length, their path ended at a large chasm. They could see that on the other side was a beautiful field of green grass. Soft beams of light bathed the field while warm, gentle breezes caressed it. It was more beautiful than anything they had ever seen before.

But there was still this frightful chasm between them and The Peaceful Place, and there was nothing now for their feet. Their whole reliance must be upon the cords, which had increased in size, until they were as large as their bodies. For a time, they were understandably distressed. They anxiously wondered, *What is the cord attached to?* They hesitated, struggling with indecision. To try to turn back would be suicide. To go forward threatened the same!

Finally, they exclaimed: "The cord is our only hope. We have depended on it all this way. It won't fail us now." Still they hesitated. Someone near the front shouted out: "God holds the cord. We don't need to fear." They passed the word along to the end of the line, adding, "He's brought us this far safely. He won't fail us now."

Finally, one at a time, they took a deep breath, grabbed their cords tightly and swung over the frightening abyss into the beautiful field beyond and were happy, perfectly happy.

Where are you in this picture? Are you just leaving the confusion? Is your trailer loaded or are you down to your shoes and socks? I'm not concerned with what your baggage is, or whether you are ahead of me or behind me on the road. I'm concerned that you're on the journey and pressing forward in it.

God is calling all of us higher, much higher. He has a legacy He wants to bestow upon us and our children. He's calling us to be men of power—each in our own realm. Will we let Him?

CHAPTER 13
JUMBLED PRIORITIES
Questions to Consider for Personal Inventory or Group Discussion

1. What are my priorities? What is most important to me? (Number 1–10 in order of importance to you.)
   a.___News/Internet
   b.___Restoring my marriage
   c.___Becoming wealthy or important
   d.___Making a living
   e.___Outreach/church duties
   f.___Sports/adventure
   g.___Finding a genuine walk with God
   h.___Entertainment/hobbies
   i.___Regaining the hearts of my children
   j._____(You fill in the blank)
2. Where do I actually invest my time and energy? What gets first attention? What gets crowded out? (Number 1–10 in order.)
   a.___News/Internet
   b.___Restoring my marriage
   c.___Becoming wealthy or important

d.___Making a living

e.___Outreach/church duties

f.___Sports/adventure

g.___Finding a genuine walk with God

h.___Entertainment/hobbies

i.___Regaining the hearts of my children

j._____(You fill in the blank)

3. Do my priorities match the way I invest my time and energy?

4. Is the tyranny of the urgent crowding out the truly essential?

5. Is my home a sanctuary or a pressure cooker?

6. Does my telephone control my time?

7. Does my TV or the Internet steal my attention?

8. Do I know the work God has called me to *in the present?*

9. What changes would God have me make?

10. When will I begin?

Men of Power

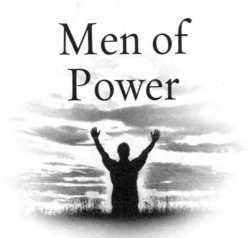

Finally, my brethren, be strong in the Lord, and in the power of his might.
—Ephesians 6:10

It's the last of the ninth, two outs, and the bases are loaded. Up to bat comes the hero of this World Series—short-stop Marty Marion. The crowd roars!

The St. Louis Cardinals, during the regular season when nobody gave them a chance to win, staged a sensational finish in the National League, winning all but nine of fifty-two games. Now, here they are in the World Series against the world champion Yankees, and the man most responsible, everyone agrees, is the Ugly Duckling short-stop, Marty Marion—the man who simply will not give up! What a man! He can't hit, but he's been hitting the ball like a demon. He would never be able to field according to the experts, but he has been fielding like an angel.

Here's the pitch. Marty sends a line drive out over second base. The runners come scampering home. Everybody's chasing the ball, but nobody's got it. Marion rounds first. The crowd is on its feet. He's heading for second. It's going to be close. Marion is safe!

Marty Marion was perhaps one of the finest heroes of baseball. He was famed as the "spark plug" of the St. Louis Cardinals—often called Mr. Short-Stop. *Wonderful* was the word everyone used to describe him. In 1945, the Philadelphia Phillies offered the St. Louis Cardinals $250,000 for short-stop Marty Marion. The Cardinals retorted that they would sooner sell the entire team than to part with their short-stop. But it hadn't always been this way.

HE'S AN UGLY DUCKLING!

Ten years earlier, one hot August day in Atlanta, crowds came to see the most promising ball player in Atlanta—not Marty Marion, but Johnny Eckles. Johnny was the star of the team, while Marty warmed the bench all season.

Johnny pleaded for the manager to give Marty a chance. "He's got persistence. He just needs to play more often."

The manager brushed him off, commenting, "He's an ugly duckling in baseball. He's skinny, awkward, and a lousy hitter. He's going nowhere!"

But Marion was Johnny's best pal, and Johnny believed in him. "Someday, he'll make it big!" he asserted.

"Forget Marion," the manager continued. "You're the one with talent. You're the best third baseman in the south, and your batting is dynamite. You ought to leave the amateurs and try out for the St. Louis Cardinals minors. The tryouts are next week. I want you to sign up for them."

Johnny went to talk to Marion and insisted that he come with him to try out for the minors. Marion thought he was crazy. Johnny insisted that if Marion wouldn't try out for the minors, neither would he.

Years before, they had made a bargain. They were buddies—best pals! Either they would make it together in minor league baseball or they would quit together. That was their pledge.

Sure, they were only kids then—twelve years old. Johnny had real talent. Marion knew he'd never be more than a bench warmer playing for a sand-lot team. No-Hit, No-Glove Marion was what they called him. Marion was determined to marry his girlfriend, Mary, and go to college.

But to Johnny, his buddy meant more to him than all the success baseball could offer. If Marion wouldn't try out, neither would he. He'd sooner go to college and stay by Marion's side than to leave his buddy out.

"Johnny, you can't do this!" Marion protested.

"I can, and I will! You know I will, too!"

"You can't throw away your big chance! Baseball is your whole life!"

"It's *our* whole life. In fact, playing baseball and marrying Mary Dellas are the only two things in the whole world you really want. I know that! So if you give it up—I give it up. That's final."

"You really mean that, don't you, Johnny!"

"I mean I want to be a ball player, and I want to go up to Rome, Georgia, next week to try out for the minor leagues. But I'm not going without you. So just choose tonight what this combination is going to do."

He hasn't got it!

Three nights later, just before Marty and Johnny were to leave for the tryouts, Mrs. Marion met Johnny alone at a restaurant. She was worried about Marty and baseball. She began, "They call him the Ugly Duckling. He can't hit. He can't field. They say he's the worst ball player in all Atlanta amateur baseball. And you're the best. Tomorrow you're both leaving for Rome for the farm club tryouts. What's going to happen to him up there when he gets the brush-off, when they laugh him off the field? What's going to happen to him inside?"

"He'll do OK," Johnny quietly replied.

"Just because you say so? He'll be hurt worse than ever. He lives and breathes baseball. He wants to play baseball, Johnny. He wants to play baseball worse than any man alive. But they say he hasn't got it."

"He'll do OK," Johnny persisted.

"He's only going up to the tryouts because you're forcing him. He couldn't live with himself knowing he'd held you back. You've been friends for so long, he couldn't bear to have you fail—to keep you back from success."

"We're pals, Mrs. Marion, ma'am. We've got a pact."

"You have a brilliant future in baseball, and he—"

"We're pals," Johnny interrupted. "If I go, Marty goes. If he stays, I stay."

"So that's the way it is."

"Yes."

"Why?" she pressed.

"I don't know. Maybe it's just because he's my friend."

"Isn't this a terribly cruel friendship you're fastening him to?"

"Perhaps."

"If not in Rome at the tryouts, it will end somewhere else. He'll be hurt. He wants to play baseball, but they say he hasn't got the talent."

"He'll get it."

"You don't get talent!" Mrs. Marion was frustrated. "And Johnny, you can't keep carrying him on your shoulders. You can't keep forcing others to make concessions to him for your sake."

"I can keep on doing what I have to do as long as I have to."

"And how long will that be?"

"Forever, if necessary."

"Why? Why are you doing this?" the concerned mother pursued. "Why are you sticking by him? It isn't just because you're his mother."

She thought a moment and said tenderly, "I love him."

Johnny persisted. "Marty Marion is my best pal. I believe in him, and you believe in him too, and that's more important than talent, don't you see? A man who has someone who believes in him is someday going to win in baseball or anything else. Because belief is a kind of love too. I know that, ma'am. Maybe he can't hit and maybe he can't field, but he's got backbone. And that's going to make up for everything he lacks. You can learn to hit; you can learn to field."

"You're a Fool!"

Johnny and Marty went to the tryouts in Rome, Georgia, and the results were as Mrs. Marion predicted. The tryout manager approached Johnny with a contract, and Johnny responded, "I can't sign with you unless you sign Marion up too."

The manager was baffled. "It must be the heat getting to me. Must be! I offer you a contract—twice—to play in the minors, and you tell me I got to sign that kid who'll never even make a good bat boy?"

Johnny asserted, "Someday, he'll be great—if someone will just stick with him. He's real stubborn and determined, and if I can just sort of buddy along with him for a while, I know he'll improve."

"You're a fool, Eckles," the manager exploded. "I've never heard of such a lame-brained, idiotic argument in my whole life. Now, boy, I'm giving you one last chance. Think what it'll be. You'll play in the minors—maybe even get called up to the majors. Now that's your dream, isn't it? Now take this pen and sign this contract."

"I can't do it!"

"Sign it! Sign it!"

"I reckon I'd better go, sir. You've been right nice to me, and I appreciate it."

"Eckles?"

"Yes, sir."

"What makes you think you're a ball player? Get out!"

As the two boys traveled home on the bus, Johnny related to Marty the parting comment of the manager, concluding, "I guess we both flunked out bad!"

Meanwhile, Mr. Rickie, the owner of the Cardinals, found out about this strange situation in Rome, Georgia. The manager told him, "Eckles is the greatest natural talent to come along in a decade. But to get Eckles, we'll have to take Marion."

The boys were shocked a few days later when they each received a telegram that read: "Leave immediately. We'll pay all expenses. Ten-day tryout. St. Louis Cardinals. Signed, Branch Rickie, General Manager."

Marty couldn't understand it. "We both got the same exact telegram. We're on our way to St. Louis. I can understand you, but why me?"

"Some dream, huh? Don't try to figure it out. Just relax."

As the two boys traveled to St. Louis, Johnny was strangely quiet. Voices echoed in his mind. *"You're a fool, Eckles." "We're pals. Years ago we made a pact. Either we make it together in minor league baseball, or we quit together. That's what we said." "He'll be hurt." "Maybe he can't hit . . . but he's got backbone. That's the most important thing." "You're a fool, Eckles, a fool." "Belief is a kind of love. A man who has someone who believes in him is someday going to win—in baseball or in anything else." "You can't keep forcing others to make concessions to him for your sake. You can't keep carrying him on your shoulders." "I can keep doing what I have to for as long as I have to." "And how long will that be?" "Forever, if necessary." "I can keep on doing what I have to . . . I can keep on doing what I have to . . . I can keep on doing what I have to."*

FORGET BASEBALL

At St. Louis, the same story was repeated—get Eckles, lose Marion. The "Gas house gang" under famed manager Frankie Frish was desperately trying to stave off the Chicago Cubs as they went down into the home stretch in a tight pennant race. Maybe Eckles could help. As for

Marty Marion, he was, according to Frankie Frish, "the worst hitter I ever saw pick up a baseball bat."

Yet, unknown to Marty, Johnny Eckles made his incredible demand. "We're buddies. It's both of us or neither."

Why it had to be that way, nobody in St. Louis understood. And before many more days had elapsed, it was the old familiar story—rejected.

Back in Atlanta, the boys decided to go to college. Marty Marion, not knowing anything about his buddy's sacrifice of his own dreams of baseball, enrolled at Georgia Tech to study mechanical drawing. The boys hung up their baseball gloves forever. Or was it?

One day the phone rang. "This is Branch Rickie. I've been thinking over this Eckles/Marion matter and I've made a decision . . . I know it's been five months . . . I know they're in college. But get them out. If we have to take Marion, we will. But get Eckles at all cost. Sign them both up to our Rochester farm team. Make sure they're both at our Florida training camp when our spring training opens. Goodbye."

That was it. He had won! Johnny Eckles had won!

Frank Rickie, the brother of the famed Branch Rickie, was later dispatched by Mr. Rickie himself to sign both boys to contracts. It was as they sat together in Tubby Walton's restaurant, or a little afterward that Marty Marion first learned of the immense confidence his pal, Johnny Eckles, had in him. He learned how Johnny had cleverly bided his time, had felt all along that he could use his own great talents to maneuver some baseball club into taking his buddy and giving him a chance. Marty Marion never forgot that courage and the absolute belief and friendship that made Johnny Eckles glad to make such a sacrifice and willing to take such a gamble.

"I'm going to make good for Johnny's sake. I'll do it. I'll never let Johnny down—never."

UGLY DUCKLING TO OCTOPUS

In the spring of 1936, because only two men were competing for a chance at short-stop, Marty Marion switched to playing short-stop. He was terrible. But he hung in there. And the rest is history.

At Rochester in 1939, he batted only .272—high for him. But he fielded flawlessly. Even when his back snapped and they had to fit him into a brace, he played 128 games in brilliant style. In 1940, the Cards called him up to the majors. By 1942, when the Cards staged a sensational pennant drive, winning 41 of their last 52 games and emerging victorious, Marty Marion had clearly become known as the team's inspired leader. In the words of Casey Stengel, "he fielded like an octopus." And "The Octopus" became his new nickname. He led the Cards to a stunning World Series upset over the New York Yankees—four games to one. In 1944, Marty Marion sparked the Cards to their third pennant in a row.

He was named the national league's Most Valuable Player. And the Ugly Duckling of baseball was now hitting his stride as he went on to become one of the greatest stars of the game.

You see, Johnny Eckles knew that Marty Marion had something far more useful than natural talent: perseverance. As Newt Rockney put it, "The man who won't be beaten, can't be beaten." The spirit that says, "I won't give up. I'll keep trying until I win" is the spirit that overcomes. It was in Marty Marion. And how generous of Johnny Eckles to sacrifice himself—encouraging Marty—to draw it out.[1]

FROM MARTY TO ME AND YOU

You and I are Marty Marion. We are the ugly ducklings—awkward, always dropping the ball and perhaps one of the worst hitters that has ever entered the game. Others may see no possibility in us. They say, "Forget him. Lose him. He doesn't have what it takes." We are tempted to give up. We are tempted to think, "I'll never make it. I'll never be anything but a bench warmer—only watching and wishing." We don't see how we could ever make it, and neither does anyone else, it seems—except for One.

Jesus is your Johnny Eckles. He is my Johnny Eckles. He is our Pal, the One with all the talent. He has said, "I will never leave you nor forsake you."[2] He believes in us against all odds and has staked His own future on His ability to make good players out of us. He believes in us; this belief is a deep love. He has pledged His life, His time, His influence to turn you and me into an octopus on the field. He wants to lead

1. Adapted from "The Ugly Duckling of Baseball," Your Story Hour cassette recording, Heritage of Our Country Series, album 6, tape H-120. Copyright 1976 Your Story Hour, Inc. Used by permission.
2. Hebrews 13:5.

us to MVP status in our marriages, our families, and our individual lives. Without Him, we'd have no chance whatsoever.

He could go on and just enjoy heaven without us. But He won't. Why? Because we are unexplainably irreplaceable to Him. He wants us to share His life and His success, and thereby find our own. He is willing to carry us on His shoulders, to do whatever it takes for as long as it takes until we get it.

Some may love us in a way that protects us from the risk of failure and rejection. Not Christ. He will expect us to attempt the impossible, to face repeated failure, to endure rejection. And He knows we will be OK through it all. Why? Because He is there for us. And His presence is enough. He knows that if we persevere with Him, we will become successful in the real game.

It is this belief in us that led Him to risk failure and infinite loss when He came to this earth as a babe, lived as a man among us, and went to the cross. He could have lost it all. But the risk was worth it to Him because we're pals and He wouldn't enjoy heaven without giving us every chance to be there with Him.

How can we disappoint Him? For His sake, let's make good. Let's determine to do it regardless of the cost to ourselves. For His sake, we can be winners.

Christ will turn us into stars at home if we learn to persevere like Marty Marion. "For the man that won't be beaten, can't be beaten." The spirit in a man that says, "I won't give up; I'll keep trying until I win" is the spirit that overcomes through Christ.

Christ is not only our Best Pal. He is our personal Coach. He has sacrificed Himself to draw us out, to bring us on the team, to turn us into men of power. He wants us to reclaim our legacy—the legacy of real manhood, the kind of manhood that leads the home team to win in the game of life—the kind of manhood your wife can truly respect and trust—the kind of manhood your sons and your daughters can safely depend on. Our legacy of real manhood will make us champions on the home field.

He's going to stick by us every day, all day, until we're transformed from the ugly duckling status into world champions. He wants us to make it *big*. To do that we must be seen as the man who simply won't give up! Perseverance, determination, follow-through must become our signatures! No longer are we going to be bench warmers! With determination and the world's best Coach behind us, let's pick up our gloves and our bats and begin addressing the real game of life. Then our wives will become our cheerleaders and our children our best fans. Someday we'll be great—because Someone is standing behind us. Jesus will stay with us as long as He has to, forever and ever if necessary. He'll never let us down— no, never! Gentlemen, we can't let Him down either—no, never!

The real game

It's the bottom of the ninth. The bases are loaded and you are up to bat. Your wife is on third, your son is on second, and your daughter is on first. Here's the pitch. The devil throws you a curve ball, but your Coach once again gives you your instruction. You send a line drive out over second base. Your runners are scampering home. Everyone's chasing the ball, but nobody's got it. You round first. The crowd is on its feet. You're headed for second and then third. On to home base! It's going to be close! Home run! You're the hero of your team. Your coach is ecstatic. Your fans are at your side. You are no longer the ugly duckling on your team. Instead, you have become the *man of power!*

CHAPTER 14
Men of Power
Questions to Consider for Personal Inventory or Group Discussion

1. In what ways do I identify with Marty Marion?
2. In what areas of my life do I feel like the ugly duckling?
3. What am I avoiding for fear of failure?
4. Am I engaged in the real game of life? Or am I participating in a substitute?
5. Do I recognize my Johnny Eckles?
6. Do I recognize the love in being asked to face hard things?
7. Will I persevere through failure and continue to try again, seeking to follow the voice of my Coach?
8. Am I becoming known as "the man who won't quit"?
9. What is the plate God is asking me to step up to?
10. Will I step up to it? When?

Want to Know MORE About the Hohnbergers?

E mpowered Living Ministries is the outgrowth of Jim and Sally's experience with God. Located near Glacier National Park, the ministry office is here to serve your needs, whether it is to book a speaking engagement, request a media appearance, or order any of a large variety of resource material including books, booklets, seminars on CD, or a special DVD series. For more information, contact:

Empowered Living Ministries
3945 North Fork Road
Columbia Falls, MT 59912

EMPOWEREDLIVINGMINISTRIES.ORG

Phone 406-387-4333
Orders 877-755-8300
Fax 406-387-4336